THE SERVICE DRIVEN LIFE™

Discover Your Path to Meaning, Power & Joy!

DONALD CLINEBELL

Praise for *The Service Driven Life*

"A privilege to read! I found myself saying a big 'yes!' to every line of *The Service Driven™ Life*. Donald Clinebell offers a unique and excellent educational and self-study guide book, introducing a revolutionary new way of discovering the path to meaning, power and joy. Through a beautifully blended form of biblical exposition, superb research, and his own spiritual experience, this compact volume provides practically and therapeutically a very resourceful tool for living—God-affirming, self-affirming, and affirming of others.

The Service Driven™ Life is an important work, a must-read companion to several of the writings of the late Dr. Howard Clinebell, the author's father. (Howard Clinebell was Professor of Pastoral Counseling at Claremont School of Theology for nearly 35 years; a world renowned author, a pioneer in the pastoral care and counseling movement; and a founding President of the American Association of Pastoral Counselors ("AAPC").)

I wholeheartedly recommend *The Service Driven™ Life!* Not only to all Christians in the world today, but to all who seek meaning, power and joy in today's broken world."

— Dr. Steve Sangkwon Shim, Ph.D. (Claremont School of Theology, 1990)
AAPC Diplomate, Executive Director, Korea Professional Psychotherapy Institute - Seoul, Korea

"*The Service Driven™ Life* is an amazing book! It is a brilliant combination of theological insight and practical guidelines for personal growth and fulfillment. This, and Donald's passion, keen intellect, and excellent writing style make this a "must read." Inspiring! Excellent for group study too.

— Rev. Dr. James King, Doctor of Rel.D
Claremont School of Theology; United Methodist Minister (Ret.), 40 years; Instructor in Sociology and Marriage and Family (Ret.), California Polytechnic State University, San Luis Obispo.

"Clinebell's book is so engaging and came to me at just the time I needed it in my life. It touched the hunger and ache in my heart for the church, for every Christian, to be fully in the world where we belong. With this book, he offers us hope, meaning and purpose in a turbulent world."

—Bishop Mary Ann Swenson
The Los Angeles Area of the United Methodist Church

The Service-Drive Life: Discover Your Path to Meaning, Power and Joy
by Donald Clinebell, J.D.

Published by HigherLife Development Services, Inc.
400 Fontana Circle
Building 1—Suite 105
Oviedo, Florida 32765
(407) 563-4806
www.ahigherlife.com

All Scripture quotations, unless otherwise indicated, are taken from the New Revised Standard Version (NRSV) © 1989 by Division of Christian Education of the National Council of the Churches of Christ in the United States of America. Used by permission.

Scripture quotations marked NKJV are taken from the New King James Version, © 1982 by Thomas Nelson, Inc. Used by permission.

Scripture quotations marked AMP are taken from the Amplified Bible, © 1954, 1958, 1962, 1964, 1965, 1987 by The Lockman Foundation. Used by permission.

Scripture quotations marked MSG are taken from The Message, © 1993, 1994, 1995, 1996, 2000, 2001, 2002 by NavPress. Used by permission.

Scripture quotations marked NLT are taken from the New Living Translation, © 1996 by Tyndale House Publishers, Inc. Used by permission.

Scripture quotations marked NASB are taken from the New American Standard Bible, © 1960, 1962, 1963, 1968, 1971, 1972, 1973, 1975, 1977, 1995 by the Lockman Foundation. Used by permission.

Scripture quotations marked JBP are taken from the J.B. Philips translation of the Bible, The New Testament in Modern English, 1962 edition, published by HarperCollins. Used by permission.

ISBN 13:
ISBN 10:

Cover Design:Principle Design Group – David Whitlock

First Edition
12 13 14—9 8 7 6 5 4 3 2 1
Printed in the United States of America.

To my parents, Howard and Charlotte, who from the beginning nourished my faith and taught me that I am filled with the capacity to love and to serve.

I love you.

Acknowledgments

The writing of this book has truly been a joyful process. The book would not have come to fruition without the good work and many talents of the men and women of faith at HigherLife Development Services: President David Welday; Product Development Manager Nikki Jenkins; Marketing Coordinator Kristin Hester; and Senior Editor C. Hope Flinchbaugh. Hope's editing skills are evident throughout the book. The marketing skills of David Whitlock and Wes Harbour have been invaluable.

I am ever grateful for the love and support of my family during this process. My parents' unconditional love and support have been present throughout. My mother, Charlotte Ellen, encouraged me and believed I had something to say. She was a very helpful sounding board during the initial drafts. My father, Howard Clinebell, instilled in me a love of learning and writing. Sadly, he did not see the book come to fruition before his "final awakening." But during my work on the book, I have often felt his presence—which has increased both my faith and my love for him.

My precious children, Brennan and Tessa, are a constant source of joy in my life. I am very proud of each of them and love them dearly. I suspect that there were times during the writing of this book that I was less available than usual. I so appreciate their understanding in that.

And finally, my heartfelt thanks to Bonnie—whom I love and adore—for believing in the importance of this work and loving and supporting me throughout.

Sometimes this book seemed to write itself. I thank God for that. And I thank God for entrusting to me the message of *The Service Driven*™ *Life* and allowing me to share it with you, the reader. May God truly bless you.

In love and service,

Donald Clinebell

San Clemente, California

Table of Contents

The only ones among you who will be truly happy are those who will have sought and found how to serve.

—Albert Schweitzer[i]

I live as a servant and thereby I am changed ... I am renewed.

—Mother Teresa [ii]

Preface

A person starts to live when he can live outside himself.
—Albert Einstein[iii]

Not long ago, I found myself standing in the self-improvement section of one of today's few popular "brick and mortar" bookstores. I was drawn by the smell of the books and distant coffee that mingled with the attractive book covers. I was struck by the sheer number of books, workbooks, audio tapes, and DVDs in this section of the bookstore, each designed to improve me. What I didn't find was help.

This book is not about self-improvement. But it can help you find what we all want—an abundant life, a life worth living. If you are looking for glib answers to unanswerable questions, this is not the book for you. If you want to get in shape, have the right journal, listen to the right tapes, walk on hot coals, have the right Blackberry or blueberry, the right iPhone or Droid or anything else, close this book now. But if you are looking for help as you address life's most important questions—or as Walt Whitman[iv] so eloquently put it: "What good amid these, O me, O life?"—then read on.

C. S. Lewis[v] once said, "We think our childish toys bring us all the happiness there is, and our nursery is the whole wide world. But something must drive us out of the nursery and into the world of others."

This book is about getting out of the nursery and moving into the world of others—not as conqueror or boss, and certainly not as a victim or rug to be trampled. *It's about emptying me of egoism—it is about leaving that lifestyle of self-absorption and self-focus—and filling our lives in service to others.* You may be reading this book at a time of personal loss, pain, sorrow, addiction, or loneliness. Or you may be grasping for joy, peace, a special relationship, or prosperity. We all want a wonderful life, but finding that place of wonder may take us to a surprising place. Are we truly willing to seek and find how to serve? Are we willing to serve others in every part of our lives—at home and in family, in vocation, and with our neighbor? Are we willing truly to live as a servant? If so, we will find our lives filled with meaning, power and joy beyond measure! I invite you to embrace the service driven life.

Introduction

In late 1976, the world seemed a bleak, self-serving place to me. I tried to find meaning in the practice of law. I tried to find meaning in a marriage—then another. And I watched, almost from outside of myself, as the storybook ending of "happily ever after" simply didn't happen. Sorrows replaced that expected happy ending: the loss of a child through miscarriage, a failed marriage. I *thought* I controlled everything, when in fact I controlled nothing. I found myself confined to a very dark place.

For me, the re-ordering of my life did not come by lightning bolt. It took time and it took work. It came step by step. And still does. The service driven life was not thrust upon me. With God's help, I chose such a life and I live life today, empowered and renewed. In fact, the service driven life has radically moved me out of that dark, confining place to a place of great joy in service.

In the pages of this book, we will explore love and service in three places:

1. Through home and family, those most precious in our lives

2. Through vocation, the way in which many hours of our days and much of our substance are spent

3. Through service for our "neighbor," in the literal and biblical senses

As we move out of self-absorption into the maturity of serving others, we gain the power to renew our minds and change, perhaps, decades of negative and controlling thinking. Although it's hard, one of the best things we can do in a time of utter darkness is to take an honest look at ourselves and ask ourselves some important questions:

- How am I of service?

- How can I be of service?

- When God stands at the door (of my heart) and knocks, do I open the door?

- Am I too busy to listen to God, or do I allow God to lead me in service to others?

At the end of each chapter in this book, you will find scripture, devotional thoughts, and questions in an effort to help you focus and implement the ideas in the chapter. I want to encourage you to take your time with these most important questions. Write about them. Pray about them. Be patient with yourself. This is *your* life, nobody else's life. Think about your journey and your path. Pray. Be still ... and ask for help, His help. He is present on your path to meaning, power and joy!

As you seek to embrace the service driven life, you may want to explore the "avenues of service" in Appendix 2. Included there are a wide array of service choices which may help you to discover your path of service. As you consider these avenues of service, beware! That tug at your heart may be something quite wonderful, something quite unexpected—it may be God moving your life!

Chapter 1

The Service Driven Life

Day breaks,

And the boy wakes up

And the dog barks,

And the bird sings

And the sap rises

And the angels sigh ...

—James Taylor[vi]

So what do you do when day breaks tomorrow morning and you'd rather not put your feet on the floor to face another day? Perhaps the song of the bird and the bark of the dog seem distant and angels a myth from childhood fairy tales. If life seems to be losing its day to day joy for you, you're reading the right book. Most likely, the answer is right in front of you but difficult to see right now.

Think of the happiest person you know—someone who seems to live life with energy, passion, and joy. Have you noticed how much time he or she devotes to serving others? How does that "happiest person" think of himself or herself? How would you describe that person's priorities? I have found that the happiest and most content person is the one who understands that the power and meaning in life is found in service.

The story is told of a life-long missionary, Mother Teresa, who for more than fifty years lived in the poverty and squalor of India helping the orphans, widows, and families who were the poorest of the poor in India. Late in her life, she was asked a simple but profound question.

"How can you live with such energy and passion in the midst of this pain and suffering?"

She answered, "I live as a servant and thereby I am changed ... I am renewed."[vii] A person who lives as a servant chooses to have no time for dark reflection, depression, fear, or self-doubt. Such a person sees meaning and purpose outside of herself, passion and joy within. Such a person finds herself with "an inner strength that survives all hurt"[viii] and readily learns to grow in relationship with other human souls and with God.

Does this mean that each of us must seek purpose and meaning in mission work in a far off land? Is every person on our planet somehow called to live a life of self-denial among pain and suffering? No. Some are called to such daily work and they are indeed angels among us.

Matthew's gospel tells this story of Jesus' first encounter with Peter and his brother:

> *As He walked by the Sea of Galilee, He saw two brothers, Simon, who is called Peter and Andrew his brother, casting a net into the sea—for they were fishermen. And He said to them: "Follow me, and I will make you fishers of men and women." Immediately they left their nets and followed Him. As He went from there, He saw two other brothers,*

James son of Zebedee and his brother John, in the boat with their father
Zebedee, mending their nets, and He called them. Immediately they left
the boat and their father and followed Him (Matthew 4:18-22).

The same story is also told in the gospel of Mark in the first days of Jesus' ministry—when He called the disciples (Mark 1:16-20).

In this story, the fishermen are called to "follow Me." They immediately, on the spot, leave their nets, their livelihoods, and their families, literally to follow Jesus as He begins His Galilean ministry. They serve Him. Does this mean that each of us is to drop everything—including our livelihood and family—to be of service? No. Or are we required to walk away from our house and vocation in order to find meaning, power and joy? No. Does it mean that the time is now to follow Him and be of service? Yes and yes!

Charles Kuralt[ix] tells the story of a seventy-eight-year-old farmer he met on the road in Virginia. Every year, the man visited a public park in the rural village where he lived. And every year, the man took vegetables grown in his own garden and left them randomly on the park's picnic tables so that there were vegetables distributed for anyone who might want or need them.

The farmer was asked, "Why do you do this?"

The farmer replied, "If you don't leave the world a better place than when you found it, what's the sense of your being here?"

The farmer was on to something, and he was not unlike the man who plants shade trees.: "A man or woman makes at least a start on understanding the meaning of human life when he plants shade trees under which he knows full well he will never sit."[x] Surely, part of the meaning of life is simply to give and to leave the world a better place than we found it. That's part of the meaning of life, but it's really only the beginning.

For most of us, our quest for meaning, empowerment, and joy in life begins when we take a hard look at ourselves and our relationship with God. Our fulfillment is found by learning to listen to God and learning to serve Him by serving others. When we truly embark upon the service driven life, we find our lives filled with meaning, power and great joy.

Chapter 2

Discover the Meaning of the Service Driven Life

"If we believe, we will learn to love,
and if we love we will learn to serve." [xi]

— Mother Teresa

"*In the beginning God . . .* (Genesis 1:1)." The meaning and power and joy of the service driven life begins with God. In order to discover the meaning of the service driven life, you must first take a hard look at your relationship with God and then understand the powerful and unshakeable connection between God and service. The key is to seek God and let Him find you as an instrument of His peace and His Will.

> *Behold, I stand at the door and knock. If any hear my voice and open the door, I will come in to him and sup with him and he with me (Revelation 3:20 KJV).*
>
> *Draw near to God, and He will draw near to you (James 4:8).*

It is imperative that we look, even right now, with love and compassion at ourselves; we need to look with compassion at our own spiritual center. If we are without a spiritual center or a spiritual core, then we are truly adrift, bereft of meaning. There is a "hole" or a vacuum within each human being that can only be filled with our spiritual center—with God. As with the fishermen in Galilee, the time is now—to follow Him.[xii]

Imagine a joyful place, a place where you are never alone—a place where all things are possible. The place you are meant to be. A place where love, compassion, redemption, forgiveness, and comfort abide.

Many of us have grown up believing that we can or should know all the answers or that at least we as humans can discover and learn all the answers. In such a worldview, accepting something—anything—on faith becomes a sign of weakness. Nothing could be further from the truth. Faith takes courage. Faith is more difficult than the absence of faith, which includes the doubt and fear that accompanies the faithless. Faith can be difficult for the human heart and mind to embrace.

In the recent movie version of *Miracle on 34th Street*, Kris Kringle tells the doubting single mother, "If you cannot accept anything on faith, you are doomed to a life dominated by doubt and by fear."[xiii]

And from the letter of the apostle James:

> *The one who doubts is like a wave of the sea, driven and tossed by the wind . . . for the doubter being doubleminded and unstable in every way (James 1:6-7).*

If we are without faith, we are unstable and double-minded. No wonder meaning and purpose are hard to find!

By contrast, "faith is the bird that sings when the dawn is still dark."[xiv] Once found, faith will abide in us and bless us, comfort, and sustain us. (See Hebrews 11:1-3.) If we truly know in faith who walks beside us at all times, we cannot experience fear and doubt. We cannot!

I am asking you now to find meaning and purpose in your life, first of all, by seeking God. Ask God for help and guidance. Pray and meditate, then pray again. Be silent and listen. Wait and listen. God wants what's best for us, but we have to want it too! Let's look again at this wonderful verse, this invitation:

Behold, I stand at the door and knock. If any hear my voice and open the door, I will come in to him and sup with him and he with me (Revelation 3:20 KJV).

Can you feel the power and promise of this passage? God stands at the door and knocks! Open the door! God's voice is heard at the door! Listen! If we answer the door, He will come in and "sup" with us.

Suddenly, in God's presence with us, we need not have all the answers. We are free and available to serve as He leads. We are enabled by His closeness to love and forgive as God loves and forgives. The meaning and power of service are unleashed in us and in others.

At some level, whether conscious or not, every man and woman on the planet seeks to know a Higher Power, something greater than him or herself—a God.

As a deer longs for flowing streams, so my soul longs for you, O God (Psalm 42:1).

Saint Augustine said that our hearts are restless until they find their way to God. How true that is! The good news is that God is near to those who call on Him in truth. (See Psalm 145:18.) Pablo Casals,[xv] world famous cellist, said, "In music, in the sea, in a leaf, in an act of kindness, I see what people call God in all these things."

Albert Einstein—a man of great genius, a man of science and rational thought—spent much time and energy exploring and writing about God and theology. Einstein was a supremely rational and scientific mind. Yet, in seeking the truth of the cosmos and its construct, he found his way, or was led, to God. Einstein reached a fascinating conclusion and "religious" endpoint:

> The highest satisfaction of a scientific person is to come to the realization that God Himself could not have arranged these connections any other way than that which does exist.

> We are in the position of a little child entering a huge library filled with books in many languages. The child knows someone must have written those books. It does not know how. It does not understand the languages in which they are written. The child dimly suspects a mysterious order in the arrangement of the books but doesn't know what it is. That, it seems to me, is the attitude of even the most intelligent human being toward God.

> To sense that behind anything that can be experienced there is something that our minds cannot grasp, whose beauty and sublimity reaches us only indirectly. In this sense, I am a devoutly religious man. [xvi]

By seeking truth in science and in the way the cosmos is constructed in a perfect "orderliness" and harmony, men and women of science often end up in "humility"—in the presence of a "magnificent structure that we can comprehend only very imperfectly."[xvii] Ironically, such a scientific analysis—in brilliant minds able to recognize a perfect and ordered harmony in the cosmos—has led many to a belief in God.

And so it was with the eminent scientist, Francis Collins.[xviii] In early 2000, Collins led a consortium of scientists who "read out" the 3.1 billion letters of the human "genome," our own DNA instruction book. Collins describes our DNA as God's language, "and the elegance and complexity of our bodies and the rest of nature as a reflection of God's plan."

In his book *The Language of God; A Scientist Presents Evidence for Belief,* Collins[xix] tells the story of his walk in the Cascade Mountains, rounding the bend to an "icefall"—a frozen waterfall "hundreds of feet high." It was at that moment—gazing upon that icefall—that the last of his "resistance to God" was "overwhelmed."

The book you are reading is not about the meaning of science or a science-driven life. It is about seeking God and letting Him find us, and seeking to serve Him in the service driven life. It is about what happens when we truly seek Him. It is about knowing that if we look for God, He will find us and lead us and transform us in service. Know this! God will never give up on you—He loves you that much. (See Luke 15:3-6.) Seek Him and let Him find you.

The book you are reading is about what happens when we truly serve and the power of service is unleashed. If we truly serve others, we cannot help but see God; He will find us.

> *You are my servant; I have chosen you ... Do not fear, for I am with*
> *you; do not be afraid, for I am your God (Isaiah 41:9-10).*

Those who do what is true come to the light. He bids us to seek Him in the still small voice, in lifting our eyes to the hills (Psalm 121), and in those magic moments of service when He moves in our lives and in the lives of those we serve. When He stands at the door and knocks, open it. And He will come in and "sup" with you and be with you in your going out and your coming in. (See Psalm 121:8.) And He will unleash in you and those around you the power of a service driven life.

If you already have a relationship with God, I invite you to embrace that relationship anew—as an instrument of His peace and His will. Feel the comfort of His presence, His guidance, the knowledge that you are not alone. "Step into the center, kneel down and let yourself be held by a forgiving God."[xx]

Seeking God

Perhaps you are seeking God for the first time. If so, you are about to go to a joyful and comforting place. Seek God and let Him find you now; in the midst of your life now, wherever you are on your path. Let Him find you as an instrument of His peace and His will. Let me share with you five ways to go to that place.

1. Seek God and let Him find you in prayer.

Seek God, and let Him find you in prayer. I love the story of Jesus in a time of prayer in the early days of His ministry. The story told in Mark 1:14-39 can help you seek God. Mark tells of the beginning of "the Galilean ministry." Jesus passed along the Sea of Galilee, where He saw Simon and his brother Andrew. Jesus called upon them to "follow me." (See Mark 1:16-18.) The brothers *immediately* left their nets and followed Jesus. Likewise, Jesus called James and John, and they left "their father . . . and followed Him" (Mark 1:19-20).

The disciples went to Capernaum, where "Jesus entered the synagogue and taught," and proclaimed the message. (See Mark 1:21.) They left the synagogue and entered the house of Simon and Andrew, where Jesus "healed many." In the midst of all of this—His teaching, His healings, His proclaiming of the message—it appears that something is troubling Jesus. And what does He do? He goes to God. How? Through prayer.

> *In the morning, while it was still very dark, He got up and went out to a deserted place, and there He prayed (Mark 1:35).*

After His time of prayer, Jesus seems to have felt renewed. He rejoins His disciples and renews His ministry with great vigor. He "went throughout Galilee proclaiming the message" (See Mark 1:36-39).

Do you feel troubled? Do you feel, lonely, sad, overwhelmed, alone? As is said in the letter of James, is someone among you suffering? Pray. (James 5:13). "Let not your heart be troubled" (John 14:1, KJV). Get up, go out to a deserted place, a place of quiet contemplation, and pray (Mark 1:36-39; James 5:13) Trust that He will find you in prayer. And that you will find yourself in a place where you can never be alone.

Through your prayer, ask for His help. "No one who has ever experienced God in prayer has ever found anything more joyful, not even owning half the world."[xxi] Seek God and let Him find you in meditation, in more prayer. He is present in the assurance that comes in a quiet moment; in the still small voice; in the injunction to "[be] still, and know that I am God" (Psalm 46:10). Even before you believe it, repeat it, out loud, again and again. There is nothing more reassuring and comforting than to discover that He was there all along.

Through prayer, ask for help. You need not have the most articulate and comprehensive prayer ever written. The content of your prayer comes from the heart, not from the words. With prayer, you say that you are willing to be helped. That you are willing to listen to and hear God's guidance—whether in the still small voice, the sheer sound of silence, or the "knowing" that appears without warning and in God's own time. In prayer, He *will* come to you. (See James 4:8.) Know it, be in it, feel it.

Spend some time "In the Company of Prayer." Consider subscribing to a daily meditation service such as this—a devotional tool to focus you on God and open you to letting Him find you.[xxii]

2. Seek God and let Him find you as you spend time in scripture.

Open a Bible. The Bible you had as a child. The Bible in the unopened drawer in the parlor. The pew Bible in the church you attend or once attended. Take in the first four words of the first chapter of the first book of the Bible: "In the beginning God ..." (Genesis 1:1). The Bible—and its sixty-six books—begins with God. The meaning and power of scripture begins with God. Feel the meaning in that, the genesis in that for you personally. Realize the origin and coming into being for you of something with great meaning, power and joy.

Feel that same meaning, power and joy in these four biblical passages:

A. First, from Revelation: "Behold I stand at the door and knock" (Revelation 3:20). Read the following three questions and pause before answering them:

   1. What form do you suppose His knock might take?

   2. Have you ever heard His knock?

   3. Are you open now to hearing God's knock—and to opening the door to a relationship with God you have never known, a relationship of great intimacy and joy?

B. Second, "[God] is near... to those who call on Him in truth" (Psalm 145:18). This powerful psalm is about truth and humility and it is about God's presence. In seeking the service driven life, you are coming to God in truth, in honesty, and in humility. Rest in the assurance that He is near you on your path. Feel how that feels. My friend, you are not alone. God is near and you can never be alone.

C. Third, from the letter of James, "a servant of God," in chapter 4, verse 8, James writes, "Draw near to God, and He will draw near to you." The book of James is quite short, 108 verses. In its opening verses, it introduces its themes: wisdom, joy, faith, blessing, endurance. In this beautifully written letter from "a servant of God," you can find much comfort, strength, and power, including the assurance that when you seek God, He will find you. He will draw near.

D. Fourth, a story of God's steadfast love and His search for you. In Luke 15:3-6 is the promise that God will never give up looking for you, finding you. He loves you that much. I give you this paraphrase from what emerges from the parable of the lost sheep:

"Which one of you, having a hundred sheep and losing one of them, does not leave the ninety-nine in the wilderness and go after the one that is lost until he finds it? When he has found it, he lays it on his shoulders and rejoices. And when he comes home, he calls together his friends and neighbors, saying to them, 'Rejoice with me, for I have found my sheep that was lost!'" (Luke 15:3-6).

Like the shepherd, God is looking for *you* and He will not stop until He has found you. He rejoices with great joy at finding *you!* God rejoices over *you!* He exults over *you!*

"The LORD your God in your midst,
The Mighty One, will save;
He will rejoice over you with gladness,
He will quiet you with His love,
He will rejoice over you with singing"(Zephaniah 3:17 NKJV).

Think about that. *Feel* that. In the words of the popular sacred song, "The Father Will Dance:"

"Is that a choir I hear, singing the praises of God?

No, the Lord God Himself is exulting over you in song!"[xxiii]

The Father will dance over you in joy. He will take delight in whom He loves! Rest in that.

The assurance of God's presence in the lives of those who seek Him is found repeatedly, in Old and New Testaments of the Bible:

"Seek the Lord ... call upon Him while He is near" (Isaiah 55:6).

"...everyone who thirsts, come to the waters.... Incline your ear and come to me... I will make with you an everlasting covenant" (Isaiah 55:1-3).

"Draw near to God and He will draw near to you." (See James 4:8; 1 Kings 8:56-57; Luke 15:3-6).

"Do not fear for I am with you; do not be afraid, for I am your God" (Isaiah 41:10).

In this section of this book, on "seeking God and letting Him find you," there is much additional scripture for prayer and meditation. There is comfort and a knowing in the Word of God, the Bible.

> *"As a deer longs for flowing streams, so my soul longs for you, Oh God"* *(Psalm 42:1).*

> *"The Lord is near to all who call on Him, to all who call on Him in truth" (Psalm 145:8).*

> *". . . I have chosen you . . ." (Isaiah 41:9-10).*

> *"I lift up my eyes to the hills… the Lord will keep your going out and your coming Inform this time on and forevermore" (Psalm 121).*

> *"Seek the Lord… call upon.Him while He is near" (Isaiah 55:6).*

> *"An everlasting covenant with you who thirst" (Isaiah 55:1-3).*

Here are a few other meditations: 1 Kings 8:56-57; Isaiah 55:1-6; Isaiah 43:1; Isaiah 41:9-10; Luke 15:3-6.

God promises to love you without condition, to be with you and lead you, comfort you, and transform you. I encourage you to spend time with these passages as you are led, before moving on in this book.

At the end of this chapter, you will find a section called "Focus on Scripture." Use it now. As you feel the need or the call, return to these scripture passages as you work through this book. Spend time reading the full context of the cited scripture. Let your reading take you to exciting and unexpected places! Let God take you to exciting and unexpected places!

3. Seek God and let Him find you as you serve.

Seek God and let Him find you as a true servant. Let Him find you—indeed speak to you—through your children in their playful laugh on a summer afternoon. Seek God and let Him find you in a quiet moment with your spouse or over a meal with family. Seek God and let Him find you in that pro bono work you are doing at work; in that unexpected moment of joy.

Many see God moving in service—in miraculous and true stories of service—in the eyes of a child in south Mexico who had never received a Christmas present, ever, until a Rotarian delivered a giant package for unwrapping. In the story of a child at-risk—mentored and tutored by one volunteer—who became a child of promise, graduating with honors and as the first college-bound child ever in her family. We can see God moving in service in the story of 7 million children walking the face of the planet polio-free because a service organization was there with a billion oral vaccines. In the story of a blind mother's sight restored following corrective surgery in a free clinic in India. Tears of joy—at seeing her own children for the first time ever! Where there is love and there is charity, God is there.

Continuous service is, quite simply, the "law of heaven."[xxiv] When you align yourself with service, you align yourself with God. And He will find you!

As you serve, remember the biblical and scriptural foundation of service. During the last supper, the night before Jesus died on the cross, He washed the disciples' feet. The Bible says in John 13:2-9 that Jesus washed the disciples' feet "as a servant to a master." And after supper, Jesus gave to the disciples a new commandment:

> "... that you love one another; even as I have loved you, that you also love one another." (John 13:34-35 RSV)

> "This is my commandment, that you love one another as I have loved you." (John 15:12)

This new commandment is not so much a command as it is an invitation—an invitation to the joy of serving God by serving others.

4. Seek God and let Him find you in recovery.

Alcoholics Anonymous and other twelve step programs are "spiritual" programs. Each of the programs, including Al-Anon—a program for those affected by the disease of alcoholism in another—is based upon the same twelve steps. AA has as its foundation "the big book," "*Alcoholics Anonymous: The Story of How Many Thousands of Men and Women Have Recovered from Alcoholism.*"[xxv] How have they recovered, and how are they recovering? By admitting powerlessness, and then by seeking and trusting God.

AA is the most successful program available for reaching and maintaining sobriety. In AA, every day of every year, recovering alcoholics seek and are found by God. They see His face; they see His will. Bill Wilson[xxvi] wrote this about alcoholism: "Without help it is too much for most of us. But there is One who has all the power – that One is God. *May you find Him now!*"

Step 2 of AA's 12-steps describes how those in recovery "came to believe in a power greater than ourselves." Step 3 describes a decision to "turn our lives over to the care of God." Indeed, six out of twelve of AA's steps make reference to God (Steps 2, 3, 5, 6, 7, 11).

The "big book"[xxvii] of Alcoholics Anonymous so eloquently describes, "What is this but a miracle of healing? Yet its elements are simple. Circumstances made him willing to believe. He *humbly* offered himself to his Maker—then he knew. To this man, the revelation was sudden. Some grow into it more slowly. But He has come to all who have honestly sought Him. We drew near to Him, He disclosed Himself to us!"

The story is told of a man who was moved to stop the drinking. One day, he did just that. A huge, almost literal, weight was lifted from his shoulders, and he heard inside him these words: "It's over. You have another chance to live." The man came to know that these were not his words. They were the words of a loving, present, and compassionate God. The man left the nursery (that C. S. Lewis talked about) and took his story in service to others. And in doing so, he discovered the meaning of a service driven life.

5. Seek God and let Him find you in your own way, in a way that God will show you.

> "Sometimes I go about pitying myself, and all the time I am being
> carried on great winds across the sky." –Ojibway[xxviii]

Let God find you in a way that is uniquely yours, in a way that God will show you. And He will, if you seek Him. Perhaps He will find you in your moment with a "beautiful and unexpected frozen waterfall, hundreds of feet high." Perhaps He will find you amidst the "majesty and beauty of God's creation" —when you kneel in the "dewy grass" and surrender.[xxix]

Or perhaps your story will be similar to that of John Wesley, founder of the Methodist Church. After a difficult and discouraging mission trip to America in 1738, Wesley was deeply discouraged and deeply in doubt about his faith. In the midst of his doubt, Wesley attended an evening worship service in the Aldersgate District of London. In his journal, Wesley describes what happened that evening:

> *In the evening I went very unwillingly to a society in Aldersgate*
> *Street, where one was reading Luther's preface to the Epistle to the*

Romans. About a quarter to nine, while the leader was describing the change which God works in the heart through faith in Christ, I felt my heart strangely warmed…I felt I did trust in Christ alone…[xxx]

That evening on Aldersgate Street, John Wesley sought God and God found Him. The comfort of God's presence was his and his life was forever changed.

Such experiences are not limited to famous scientists and founders of the faith. If you seek God, He *will* find you, in a way that God will show you. I want to encourage you not to feel rushed or pushed, but to spend time implementing the ideas in this chapter and using the scriptural focus and the questions for "writing and prayer" that follow this chapter. Be patient with yourself. Take your time before moving to the next chapter. God wants a relationship with you that is both personal and intimate in a way you likely have never known. Be open to that. The rewards, the comfort, the meaning, the power—all given to you that you may find great joy, unimaginable in common days.

Be Open, Hear His Voice

As you seek God, it is important to "let Him find you." It could be that over the years you've had a kind of cosmic spiritual sense that "I didn't create myself" and that some spiritual force did. That's a start, a spiritual start, but know that's not where you want to stay. God loves you and wants to enjoy a personal and intimate relationship with you— know that He is there, He is present, and eager to "find" you, if you are open to it.

I don't know how many times I've been given what I have come to call the "shower solution." Faced with a problem that seemed impossible to solve, an obstacle that seemed insurmountable, I worked the problem in my head. I worked it some more. And when it seemed there was no solution, I worked it some more. Then, without warning, perhaps in the shower or some other odd place or moment, suddenly the solution was there and that "knowing" was in front of me. Of course, that's a tremendous relief when you've been wrestling with something. "Oh, yes, that's it!" I've said in response.

What I have come to know over time is that God speaks to me in ways to which I am not always open. When I am open, He leads me and guides me. Now, instead of responding with, "Oh yes, that's it," I offer up a simple and heartfelt praise: "Thank you, God!"

When I am not open to Him, I do not hear Him. But He is still speaking! He is still there to lead me and guide me and help me when I am ready. I encourage you, no matter your "religious" background, to be open to hearing His voice. Perhaps He speaks to you when you walk or run in the morning or maybe He whispers to you in the quiet stillness of the night. I know a man who keeps a tablet and pen next to his bed for those middle of the night "wake-ups" when a thought or idea is suddenly "right there." The man said, "I used to simply go back to sleep, 'til I learned it wasn't my idea or solution at all! It was God's words, His idea, His solution! Once I learned that, boy, did I get up in a hurry. And boy, did I write things down."

That sudden solution you've experienced in the face of an ongoing and difficult problem? Be open to the fact that the sudden "knowing" you felt was not your brain firing better today than yesterday or the result of that extra cup of coffee, or even more or better rest. That meeting with a certain person in your life, at a certain time in your life, that seems now to have been an extraordinary coincidence? Be open to the fact that that wasn't coincidence at all! That was God.

I am as convinced as I can be that more people refuse to hear God's voice, and indeed, deny the presence and even the existence of God through the use of the word "coincidence" than in any other way. Think about your life. Think about the times you have exclaimed, "What a coincidence!" Maybe not.

There is out there an old expression: "Listen to your heart." It's most commonly used to advise listening to "you," to "your truth." Is it possible that when you listen to your heart, you are listening to God working through you? Be open to that. If you are, you will know.

If you are open to Him, you will hear His voice. The passage in Revelation 3:20 assures you that He is speaking to you. "Behold I stand at the door and knock. If *you* hear my voice and open the door I will come in to *you* ... " Verse 20 does not say, "If I happen to be speaking and you hear My voice ..." No, it says, "If you hear My voice." His voice is at the door! He is speaking to you! Listen for Him in the everyday sounds around you; perhaps you will be captured by a sudden awareness of His grace, His gift to you of love and compassion.

If you are open to Him, you *will hear* His voice. Perhaps it will be in a time of creativity—when you touch the eternal in you through poetry, writing, or music. Perhaps you will hear His voice in a time of song, when God will put a "new song" in your mouth and your heart. (See Psalm 40:3.) Or you may hear

Him clearly speak to you amidst the majesty and beauty of God's creation.

Perhaps you will hear God speak to you during a time of difficulty, a time of great pain and hurt in your life. If you are open to the way in which God speaks to you—in the quiet "knowing," in the still small voice—you can find in God a place of calm in the midst of great difficulty. Earlier in this chapter, I told the story of a man who was "moved" to stop drinking and that weight was lifted from his shoulders. That man came to know that those simple words he had "heard" that day were not his. They were God's.

I once found myself in the midst of great pain, following a huge change in my life, for which I was unprepared and which was not in accordance with "my will." It was a lonely time—a frightening time. C. S. Lewis would call such a moment "a time of suffering." One day, I was walking along the ridgeline of an idyllic, rain-drenched foothill, taking in the beauty, but in a place emotionally of great loneliness. An eagle circled overhead and dropped gradually lower and lower. I was fixated on its flight, unable to look away. The eagle swooped down from the sky, layer by layer, and finally lighted upon a barren and grizzled tree to the side of the road. I was awed. Speechless. All of a sudden, there came to me five words: "It's going to be okay." I was surprised at the words—they didn't feel like mine. I wasn't even sure I believed them. But I also felt an enormous calm wash over me as I stood on that path. Was I alone with that eagle? No. I was not. I was with an eagle and I was with God. The eagle did not speak to me. God did, and I heard it.

In times of great difficulty, pain, suffering, addiction, or loneliness, be open to hear His voice. There is a wonderful book titled *God Calling*.[xxxi] It was written by two women—anonymously. Nowhere in the book do the names of the writers appear. In the preface to the book, the two women are simply identified as "two listeners." God called to "two lonely women," they listened, and were led to write down what they heard God say to them. One of the two listeners wrote about what she had learned: "That God speaks today, plans and guides the humblest, that no detail is too insignificant for His attention, that He reveals Himself now as ever as a Humble Servant and majestic Creator." Yes, He speaks today; not loudly, not rumbling from behind a bush. No. Quietly He speaks. Quietly, powerfully, and with the assurance of His presence and His guidance and His comfort.

If you are open to Him, you *will* hear His voice. In times of great trial, He will comfort you.

"Blessed are those who mourn, for they shall be comforted" (Matthew 5:4).

"Weeping may endure for a night, but joy cometh in the morning"
(Psalm 30:5 KJV).

Hear His Voice, Open the Door

I opened chapter two with the promise of Revelation chapter three. Nowhere is God's assurance and invitation clearer and more powerful than this chapter in the last book of the Bible. Let's look at the fullness of what God offers you in this passage. "Behold, I stand at the door and knock" (vs. 20). God is knocking at *your* door and He is speaking to *you!* "If you hear my voice ... " (vs.20). Seeking God and letting Him find you is about hearing His voice and then opening the door. No matter your story or your circumstances, how long you've waited or how far you have moved away from God, He is still knocking. Whether you open the door through prayer or scripture, through service or recovery, or in a way that God will show you, I encourage you to open it!

And what would happen if you opened the door? "If you hear my voice, and open the door, I will come in to you and sup with you and you with me" (vs. 20). When you hear His voice and open the door, God will come in to you! And He will sup with you, He will eat with you and you with Him. I submit to you that the use of the "meal" as an image in verse 20 is not an accident. A meal together means an opportunity for intimacy—a time to be nourished and a time when those who partake can truly communicate with each other. Even in our busy culture, people can truly connect with each other over a meal and seek true intimacy and communication. Indeed, there is much research to support the powerful effect upon families who "sup" together regularly.

What happens in families where meals are taken together? There is much evidence that in such families, children achieve more in school, substance abuse is lessened, the divorce rate is lessened, and true intimacy in the family is more likely. Families whose members spend time in each other's company, who slow down and engage with each other, are likely to find that the family meal helps to anchor the family. That special time around a table together provides a point of connection with each other and with God.[xxxii]

In this beautiful image given us in Revelation, God seeks an intimate relationship with you. He wants a closeness, a nearness, an inseparability. God seeks an intimate relationship with *you*—beyond anything you have ever known. In a very real way, when you seek Him, He will find you. Hear His voice at the door, open the door and He will sup with you and you with Him. What does that mean? It means this:

That all things are possible through Him (Philippians 4:13)

That He will love you, through the gift of His grace, without condition. (John 15:9; 1 John4:7-16; John 3:16.)

That salvation—love and forgiveness—comes by God's grace alone (Romans 3:19-28; Ephesians 2:8-9; Titus 2:11)

That He will be with you (Psalm 23:4, 6; Psalm 73:23; Revelation 3:20; James 4:8; Luke 15:3-6; Psalm 145:18; Isaiah 41:9-10; Genesis 9:8-17; Matthew 18:20; Matthew 28:20; John 6:37; Romans 8:38-39)

That He will guide you and lead you (Psalm 23:1-3; Hebrews:13:6; Psalm 73:24; Psalm 139:9-10; Psalm 46:11; Psalm 48:14; Revelation 3:20; Exodus 15:13; Isaiah 41:13)

That He will abide in you (1 John 4:16)

That He will comfort you (2 Corinthians 1:3-4; Isaiah 66:13; Psalm 71:20-21; Psalm 121:1,-2, 5; Isaiah 40:31; Psalm 40:1, 11, 17; John 14:1-2; John 14:27; Jeremiah 31:13)

That He will transform you (2 Corinthians 5:17; Isaiah 55:1-6; 1 Kings 8:56-58; Revelation 3:21.)

That He will "keep your going out and your coming in from this time on and forevermore." (Psalm 121:8.)

In the life-changing words of the First Letter of John:

"So we have known and believe the love that God has for us. God is love, and those who abide in love, abide in God, and God abides in them" (1 John 4:16).

Stop and drink in these beautiful and gentle words. Your path to purpose and meaning is founded upon your relationship with God, upon the comfort and assurance of your faith. As Jesus said to the disciples in the upper room on the night before His death, "I am the way, and the truth, and the life" (John 14:6). "Believe in God, believe also in me. In my Father's house there are many rooms" (John 14:1, RSV).

Earlier in this chapter, we looked at the truth that God seeks an intimate relationship with *you*—beyond anything you have ever known. A relationship in which He is present, guiding you and leading you, comforting you, transforming you. Let's recall now the powerful yet gentle story of God and the "Footprints in the Sand":

> *One night I had a dream – I dreamed I was walking along the beach with the Lord and across the sky flashed scenes from my life. For each scene I noticed two sets of footprints in the sand. One belonged to me and other to the Lord. When the last scene of my life flashed before me, I looked back at the footprints in the sand. I noticed that many times along the path of my life there was only one set of footprints. I also noticed that it happened at the very lowest and saddest times of my life. This really bothered me and I questioned the Lord about it.*

> *"Lord, you said that once I decided to follow You, You would walk with me all the way. But I have noticed that during the most troublesome times in my life, there is only one set of footprints. I don't understand why in times when I needed you most, you should leave me." The Lord replied: "My precious, precious child, I love you and I would never, never leave you during your times of trial and suffering. When you saw only one set of footprints, it was then that I carried you."* [xxxiii]

Seek Him and let Him find you. Abide in Him. He will not fail you. All is well. Courage!

God and Service

> *"A new commandment I give you, that you love one another; even as I have loved you, that you also love one another" (John 13:34-35 RSV).*

> *"Those who do what is true come to the light... their deeds have been done in God" (John 3:21).*

In the first part of this chapter, I emphasized that we need to seek and be found. We all need to seek a relationship with God that is filled with God's promise and assurance, by His compassion, redemption, and forgiveness; a relationship centered upon His nearness, His inseparability from us, and His unconditional love for us. To embrace fully the meaning of the service driven life, we must understand the powerful and unshakeable connection between God and service.

Service as a way of living, even a commandment for living, transcends every form of religion, including the world's largest religion, Christianity. It does not transcend God. Even Webster, when defining the word "service," ends up with God! Webster's New World Dictionary says that *service* means "Occupation of a servant, of one who serves. Work done or performed for another; an act giving assistance or advantage for another. Outside of self. Outside of ego. Serving God through good works."[xxxiv]

The Church's One Foundation: Service

There is, of course, a well-known hymn, the music penned by Samuel Wesley, in the 1800s. Let's look at just the first and the sixth verses. The sixth verse, in particular, has to do with the communion and special relationship that God desires to have with us.

Verse 1

The Church's one foundation

Is Jesus Christ her Lord,

She is His new creation

By water and the Word.

From heaven He came and sought her

To be His holy bride;

With His own blood He bought her

And for her life He died.

Verse 6

Yet she on earth hath union

With God the Three in One,

And mystic sweet communion

With those whose rest is won,

With all her sons and daughters

Who, by the Master's hand

Led through the deathly waters,

Repose in Eden land.

The lyrics in the first verse commence with the statement that the church's one foundation is Jesus Christ our Lord. The church is "His creation by water and the Word."xxxv And who can doubt the power and the joy that underlies such a hymn!

But having seen the classic understanding of the "church's one foundation," it is important to go the next step. On the night before He was crucified, Jesus washed the disciples' feet "as a servant to a master" (John 13:3-9). And He gave His disciples a new commandment: To "go and do as I have done."

Love [others] as I have loved you (John 15:12 Also John 13:34-35).

The foundation of the Christian faith is service: service to God through service to others. Christians are commanded to serve and enjoined to love God and love others as God loves us. The two greatest commandments, said Jesus of Nazareth, are to love God with all your heart, soul, and mind and strength and to love one another—love your neighbor. (See Mark 12:28-31; Luke 10:25–28.) We are sent to serve. (See 1 Peter 4:10.)

Love [others] as I have loved you (John 15:12; John 13:34-35).

For I was hungry and you gave Me food, I was thirsty and you gave
Me something to drink, I was a stranger and you welcomed Me, I was
naked and you gave Me clothing, I was sick and you took care of me. .
(Matthew 25: 31-46). As the Father sent me, I send you.

After this the Lord appointed seventy others and sent them on ahead
of him to every town and place where He himself intended to go...he
Kingdom of God has come near. (Luke 10:1-11). Go where He would
go and do what He would do. As you have seen in me, do the same.

Little children [meaning all of us], let us love, not in word or speech,
but in truth and action (1 John 3:18).

Let no one seek his own good, but the good of his neighbor.
(1 Corinthians 10:24).

"Preach the gospel at all times, and when necessary, use words." – St. Francis of Assisi[xxxvi]

We are sent to "make humankind our business; the common welfare is our business; mercy, charity and forbearance are our business." (Charles Dickens, *A Christmas Carol*.)

Whoever wishes to become great among you must be your servant (Mark 10:43).

If you had faith the size of a mustard seed…would you not rather say to him, 'Prepare supper for me, put on your apron and serve me while I eat and drink.' (Luke 17:5-10). If you would be great…serve.

In Christian terms, we empty ourselves, as Jesus did. We serve God by serving others. The imperative to serve is also woven throughout the Bible's Old Testament.

I therefore command you, 'Open your hand to the poor and needy neighbor in your land' (Deuteronomy 15:11).

And what does the Lord require of you but to do justice, and to love kindness, and to walk humbly with your God (Micah 6:8).

Deuteronomy 11:13 and 1 Samuel 12:20 admonish the believer to love and serve with all of our heart and soul. And, of course, there is the prophet Isaiah's vision and call to service:

Whom shall I send, and who will go for us?… Here I am, Lord; send me (Isaiah 6:8).

God is present in the midst of your service. Isaiah 41:9-10 tells us that He will strengthen, uphold, and help you.

What Service Does Not Mean

A brief word about what service is not. Service here is not a means by which we "work" ourselves into some eternal reward. Rather, it is about lives lived with purpose, meaning, power and joy—lives lived with God.

The popular Christian culture—even the "best-selling" kind—has done little to address the true meaning and power of service and the service driven life. Unfortunately, in some cases, the most popular Christian spiritual leaders have, by design or otherwise, done harm. Indeed, it is sometimes written that God commands us to serve and that He will judge those who do not serve. If God is unhappy with our service, so the story goes, He will pour out His anger upon us. Some authors even predict the loss of eternal rewards for those who live for themselves, who do not serve.[xxxvii] Thus, we are introduced to fear and guilt. Neither fear nor guilt is a basis for finding peace and meaning!

In the Christian faith, salvation, love, and forgiveness come by God's grace. It is free, not gained by "works," and it, in turn, frees us to love and forgive and to serve as Jesus served. (See Romans 3:19-28; Ephesians 2:8-10; Titus 2:11.) Even faith is not a condition of receiving the gift; faith is, rather, a sign of the gift already given.

The Antidote for Fear and Guilt: Amazing Grace

The antidote for fear and guilt? His grace. God's gift is either free or it is not. And it most assuredly is—through His amazing grace. The well-loved hymn, *Amazing Grace*, is one of the most recognized in the English speaking world. It has been recorded multiple thousands of times. It is estimated that worldwide the hymn is performed 10 million times each year.[xxxviii] Why? Aside from its gorgeous, yet haunting melody, perhaps the constancy of its performance is explained by this: It contains in its lyric a fundamental truth about God and about our relationship with God. Consider the story of John Newton, the man who wrote the words to the hymn we now know as Amazing Grace.

Amazing Grace[xxxix] is often referred to as a white spiritual. But it is not. The words to this amazing hymn were written in 1779 by John Newton. Newton was white. If one looks at most Protestant hymnals, the music is attributed to "unknown." In fact, history records that Newton first heard the melody which later became known as *Amazing Grace* on a slave ship—a melody haunting, yet inspired, emanating from the depths of that slave ship as it traversed the Atlantic. As the remarkable bass/baritone Wintley Phipps[xl] says before each of his performances of *Amazing Grace*, "When I get to heaven, I want to meet that slave named 'unknown.'"

One night in 1779, while aboard that slave ship, a terrible storm arose. Newton was frightened and called out to God. Thus began his spiritual conversion. His career in slave trading ended a few years later and he began studying theology. He was later ordained in the Church of England, and began to preach and to write. The lyrics to *Amazing Grace* were written by this self-proclaimed "wretch"—to illustrate one of his sermons. When the lyrics were put to the melody, the hymn became known as *Amazing Grace*, bringing a message of unconditional forgiveness and redemption, regardless of the gravity of sin and regardless of works—a message of true grace. Grace that finds us:

Amazing Grace, how sweet the sound,

That saved a wretch like me

I once was lost, but now am found,

Was blind but now I see.

Twas grace that taught my heart to fear

And grace my fears relived

How precious did that grace appear

The hour I first believed.

Yea, when this flesh and heart shall fail,

And mortal life shall cease

I shall possess within the veil

A life of joy and peace. "[xli]

This grace "leads us home" "within the veil" to a life of joy and peace.

You can seek God and be found by God. When you are found, you will experience a God of comfort and a God of grace for you; a God with the gift of love, compassion, redemption and forgiveness. Grace that "leads you home" "within the veil"—to a life "of joy and peace."

For now, we leave theological conundrums aside, for a life-changing invitation awaits. The meaning of the service driven life is found in its spiritual base—in its connection (*your* connection) to God. We are commanded to serve, and as you will see in the chapters that follow, we find in that commandment an invitation to empowerment and great joy!

Stories of Service

At the end of chapters 2 through 4 of this book you will find true stories of service—each filled with meaning, power and great joy. Spend some time considering how others serve and how others are changing their own lives and the lives of those they serve. With each story, ask yourself these questions:

- *How does the story affect me?*
- *Does the story speak to me? How so?*
- *Do I see God moving in these stories of service?*

Be still. Listen. He will lead you in His time. Trust Him.

In the two stories that follow this chapter, think about two things:

1. God finds those who serve.

2. Where love and service are present, there is God. Therein lies the meaning and the power of service.

The Surgeon/Sight to the Blind[xlii]

I know the true story of a young mother in India, age 29, blind her entire life. She had two children—a six-year-old boy and a four-year-old girl. A surgeon from the United States took the time and the energy to care. Working through a service club in India, the surgeon gathered and sent surgical instruments and equipment to India and assembled a surgical team of volunteers. On a January day, the surgical team took to the air and flew some 8000 miles—from the United States to India—to perform without charge an amazing and life-changing surgery.

The surgery was delicate, risky, and difficult. After ten hours of surgery and hours upon hours of recovery, the mother slowly opened her eyes and began to weep. Not just because she could see for the first time, but because for the first time ever ... she laid eyes upon her son and daughter, ages six and four.

Yes, the tears of joy in the young mother were shared by tears of joy in the surgeon who later said this: "I believe I know how the surgery changed that young mother and those two children. But what I know without doubt is that *I* am changed. I do what I do with God's help. And in that mother and in those children, I have seen the face of God."

The Adoptive Parents/Kids HIV Positive[xliii]

Jesus called for them and said 'Let the little children come to me, and do not stop them; for it is to such as these that the kingdom of God belongs.' (Luke 18:16).

Countless children in Ethiopia and throughout the third world are born HIV positive and lose their parents to AIDS. The sentence for these kids: to live orphaned in Ethiopia in unthinkable poverty with an early death sentence. A married couple, Kiel and Carolyn Twietmeyer, living in the U.S. with seven birth children, adopted in the US six Ethiopian children, and found Project Hopeful. Within a very few years, the project is placing in loving homes in the US thousands of HIV positive children from many different countries and is advocating on behalf of such kids everywhere.

When asked about the program, Carolyn said this: "God strengthened me to do this. What is amazing is what God is able to do with our 'yes.' What God has done for us!" And from Kiel: "God used my wife ... I learned to lean into God. God dealt with me about caring for these kids. And God has richly fulfilled our lives with and through these wonderful kids."

Implementing the Ideas in This chapter

Focus on Scripture

In the beginning God (Genesis 1:1).

Behold, I stand at the door and knock (Revelation 3:20 KJV).

God is near to those who call on Him in truth (Psalms 145:18).

So He told them this parable: Which one of you, having a hundred sheep and losing one of them, does not leave the ninety-nine in the wilderness and go after the one that is lost until he finds it? When he has found it, he lays it on his shoulders and rejoices! (Luke15:3-6)

Draw near to God and He will draw near to you (James 4:8).

Love [others] as I have loved you (John 15:12).

Please go to Appendix 1 of this book for additional focus on scripture and to encourage you on your path to meaning, power and joy.

Reflections

"Ubi caritas et amor."

"Where there is love and charity, God is present." (Gregorian chant)[xliv]

"I am with you. Do not fear. Never doubt My love and power."[xlv]

Chapter Review

Focus on these specific ways—covered in this chapter—to seek God and let Him find you. If you think it would be helpful, return to each of these topics in the chapter.

- Seek God and let Him find you in prayer.
- Seek God and let Him find you as you spend time in scripture.
- Seek God and let Him find you as you serve.
- Seek God and let Him find you in recovery.
- Seek God and let Him find you in your own way, in a way that God will show you.
  - *Be open, hear His voice.*
  - *Hear His voice, open the door.*

Focus on the powerful and unshakeable connection between God and service. If you think it would be helpful, return to each of these topics in the chapter:

- The Church's one foundation: service
- What service does not mean
- The antidote for fear and guilt: amazing grace

Questions to Write and Pray About

Can I be open to God granting me the courage to take a deliberate step of faith?

_____

_____

_____

Have I ever experienced peace in my life?

_____

_____

_____

Have I ever experienced the absence of fear in my life, even for a moment?

_____

_____

_____

Have I ever thought I "felt" the presence of a higher power?

_____

_____

_____

Have I ever seen God move in my life or in the lives of others? Where? When?

_____

_____

_____

Do I truly believe that if I seek God He will find me?

_____

_____

_____

Have I ever felt God in a quiet moment?

_____

_____

_____

Can I be still and let Him find me as an instrument of His peace and His will?

_____

_____

_____

How would it feel to me to "open the door" and "sup" with God and He with me?

_____

_____

_____

Can I embrace the power of the connection between God and service?

_____

_____

_____

Can I let go and trust God…and feel His presence and His peace and His grace?

_____

_____

_____

Chapter 3

Discover the Power of the Service Driven Life

After we seek out a new, intimate, and loving relationship with God and we understand the unshakeable connection between God and service, we are ready to take two powerful steps toward the service driven life:

1. Change our thinking

2. Change our priorities

God knows us well and He knows how to "personalize" His work of change so that each of us is ministered to according to who we are and even according to our own style of learning. God made us. He knows how to help us in both of these steps so that we will be changed in a way that will open us, free us, and bring us to experience the "joy without measure"—the "complete" joy of living the service driven life.

Change Your Thinking

> *"If you keep on saying things are going to be bad,*
> *you have a good chance of being a prophet."*
> *– Isaac Singer*[xlvi]

How Do You Think of Yourself?

This chapter is about you. It is about change in you. It is about changing your thinking in a very powerful way. What goes on in the six inches between your ears? When you think about your life and the meaning of what you do, are you defeated before you begin?

Do you see what you do every day as meaningless, worthless, hopeless? Do you think of yourself as unworthy, lacking in goodness, filled with nothing but flaws and defects of character? If so, that kind of thinking locks you in a very dark and lonely room, full of fear, doubt, and self-judgment. Your thinking can control and smother you; it can sap every bit of meaning, power and joy from your life. Are you living a life of "quiet desperation?"[xlvii] Are you living a life filled with fear? If so, that's okay; know that you are not alone. Others have felt that, too.

The trouble with such thinking is not just its impact upon you, although that's devastating enough. Such thinking in you also impacts all those with whom you come in contact—especially those closest to you—those with whom you spend time; those with whom you want closeness and intimacy;

indeed, those most precious to you. If you live in fear, doubt, and self-judgment, there is at least one guarantee: those near you will know it and see it! They will know it and see it in your misdirected anger, your judgment of others, your sarcasm, your resentments, and perhaps, your depression.

You see, love and fear are inconsistent with one another. Let's see what the Bible says in the First Letter of John:

There is no fear in love. But perfect love drives out fear, because fear has to do with punishment. The one who fears is not made perfect in love (1 John 4:18).

If you live in fear, that fear is likely to eclipse the very center of your love and compassion for yourself and others. Conversely, a life filled with God's love—love for yourself, for God, and for others—is a life that has little room for fear. "Love over fear" is not just a slogan. It is a choice. You can choose to abide in love and thus abide in God—and He in you.

Whoever lives in love, lives in God, and God in him. In this way, love is made complete among us so that we will have confidence…because in this world we are like Him (1 John 4:16-17).

The good news is that your thinking can control and smother you or *it can free you!* Are you living a life filled with love and compassion, a life of love over fear? Are you living a life filled with power and passion? Do you think of yourself as fundamentally good—as loving and compassionate, filled with the capacity to forgive? Do you truly believe that what you do is worthy? Do you see that everything you do—*everything*—is, or can be, a vessel for service? If you struggle with some of these questions, here are some steps to consider that will help you to think in a way that will do nothing less than free you.

Accept and embrace God's unconditional love, forgiveness & redemption.

In chapter two, we talked about seeking God and letting Him find you. It's important to realize that God wants a personal and intimate relationship with each of us. He desires nearness, closeness, an inseparability from you. He will never stop looking for you. (See Luke 15:3-6.) God offers through His grace the gift of unconditional love, forgiveness, and redemption for you. (See Isaiah 55:1-6; Isaiah 43:1; Luke 15:3-6; Romans 3:19-28; and Ephesians 2:8-9.) If you hear His voice and you open the door, He will come in to you and sup with you, offering His love, His presence, His comfort,

His peace (Revelation 3:20). You will find great freedom as you accept and embrace His love—even now, as you hold this book in your hands! Come to know Him as did the apostle John:

So [I] have known and believe the love that God has for [me] ..." (1 John 4:16.)

You may want to revisit chapter two where we talked about seeking God and letting Him find us. (If you are wondering if you've fully entered into this, you may want to look at the questions at the end of chapter two.)

Have you long thought that God was not there, or at least not there for you? Again, you aren't alone. But it is time, right now, to change that thinking. My friend, have faith. He is there. He is speaking to *you*, perhaps in ways you've not yet heard or recognized. Hear His voice, open the door to Him. (Again, see Revelation 3:20). If we draw near to God, He will draw near to us. (See James 4:8.) Feel His presence and accept the gift of His love and forgiveness through His grace, without condition. (See Romans 3:19-28 and Ephesians 2:8-9).

He will never leave you, nor forsake you (Hebrews 13:5).

It may feel silly, but I recommend you say that last scripture verse out loud: "He will never leave me, nor forsake me." Repeat the sentence out loud. Try to say it without smiling! Be conscious of what you feel as you say these words out loud and those of the apostle John in Revelation and the letter of Paul to the Romans. Put a "feeling word" to what you are feeling. Do you feel happy, free, relieved, content, comforted, or joyous? Accept and embrace the power of God's love and presence. I encourage you to do it now! If you've not experienced God's love, forgiveness, and redemption before, you've lived without it long enough. It is time!

Love and forgive yourself as God loves and forgives you.

Loving and forgiving yourself as God does will revolutionize your thought process. However, you may find it difficult to change your thinking. This is a change, a re-ordering, which, for many of us, requires a fundamental shift in the way we have thought and lived for decades. I encourage you to be patient and kind with yourself; it takes time to effect this change. This is a change in your thinking which you may never have contemplated. But if you stick with it, the rewards are many and rich—in energy, passion, power, and, ultimately, joy.

Oscar Wilde once said that "to love oneself is the beginning of a lifelong romance."[xlviii] For some of us, our view of our own lives and our own selves has kept us in that very dark room I talked about earlier. Some of us are fighting against ingrained ways of living and thinking that have occupied us for decades—ways of living and thinking that we learned and learned well as children.

There is much in our past and in our lives over which we simply have no control. What we come to learn over time is that we *do* have control over our own attitudes and our own thinking. And that it is not only okay, but it is essential that we change our attitudes and thinking by learning love and compassion for ourselves. Thoughts of judgment and self-loathing *can* be changed. Such thoughts do not comprise who we are. Over time, we come to learn and accept some fundamental truths about ourselves. Here are a few thoughts that may be new to you, but you can practice when you look in the mirror:

> *I am not perfect, but I am making progress.*
> *I live a life filled with love and compassion and forgiveness—for me!*
> *In that love and compassion and forgiveness for me I am freed.*

More on the power of that freedom in a moment.

While these truths may at first seem strange, perhaps almost foreign, that means only this: that you have effectively cut yourself off from the truth about yourself. But as a shift in thinking occurs, this place of love and compassion and truth will yield extraordinary bounty. Are you ready to try this again? Find a place where you feel comfortable reading out loud. Here we go!

> *I am not a man or woman who gets up in the morning and accomplishes nothing; hates my work; has nothing to offer to those I love or to the world. No! I am a source of goodness, love, compassion, forgiveness, serenity, and peace. I am imperfect, but I am God's creation! I am created in the image of God (Genesis 1:27-28) and I am therefore good (Genesis 1:31), and filled with the capacity to love and to serve!*

Yes! Yes, I am!

Freed to love and forgive others as God loves and forgives you.

The most effective people on the face of the planet are not those with the best personal digital assistants, the most updated Blackberry or Palm Pilot or notebook, the right I-device, or the latest invention from the mind of Bill Gates or the late Steve Jobs. No, the most effective, happy, and content people on the planet are quite simply those who see themselves as serving others. They see what they do as a means of service. They see everything—yes, everything—they do as a means of service. They find in what they do a means to serve others. They find meaning, power joy, and passion in what they do and how they do it. It is in this sense that their thinking determines the outcome, when they come face to face with that most difficult question: "What does it mean?"

"The true measure of a man (or woman) has nothing to do with status; life is not about prestige; it is about passion and purpose. It is about impacting the lives of others." [xlix] And understanding that everything you do—yes, everything—is, or can be, a vessel for service.

It has been said that the truest and purest act of service is in loving another unconditionally and with compassion. Many never reach this place of true service because they are unwilling to look at themselves and their thinking about themselves. As Carl Jung said: "Your vision will become clear only when you can look into your own heart"[l]. Those who sit in fear, self-doubt, and depression will not care for themselves or others. They will find it is not "on their radar" to serve others and flounder at trying to find the power of a service driven life. To move to a new place, a powerful place of truth and strength, takes courage. Sit with it. Make a beginning. Take a step. Re-read this chapter if need be, concentrating on how it feels.

Sit quietly with your children, with your spouse, with a person close to you. Be still and know that there is help and comfort always available—in professional settings, in recovery settings, and in an ever-present God who knows your name and knows who you are. (See Isaiah 43:1 and Jeremiah 1:5.) Consider the truth that God loves you without condition, just as you are. Let it become your new reality. Accept and embrace Him and His grace in all its splendor and glory. Do it, now!

I spoke in chapter two about seeking God and letting Him find you in prayer. Now, through prayer, let Him help you and guide you in your thinking. Take a few minutes to pray through the questions following this chapter and jot down some of your thoughts. Most of all, give yourself the gift of love and compassion. Love yourself as God loves you and watch what happens at home, at work, and in your life. Ultimately, if you love yourself as God loves you, you will impact the lives of those you encounter every single day.

Remember that it is your thinking that either hinders or releases the true power of service. It is within your control to find your servant mind and heart and to find a means to serve others. Practice seeing yourself as serving others as a man or woman of God. It is in this sense that *your thinking* determines the outcome.

Over time, as you implement the ideas in this chapter, you will come to re-order your thinking in a way that points you toward the power of the service driven life.

The shift is difficult, but the rewards are immense and unlimited and powerful beyond measure. As your thinking shifts, you will be astounded at the opening of the floodgates and the flow of love and compassion for your spouse, for your children—for those most precious to you—and for other human souls. Such a shift in thinking can free you to love others as God loves you, with a love deep and rich in power and joy. Of course, this shift will bring peace and contentment to you as well.

Love God; think of yourself as a man or woman of God.

The gospel of Mark tells the story of the scribe (or writer) who "came near" and heard a group of "Sadducees" disputing Jesus. (The Sadducees, from the Hebrew *Tsdoki,* meaning "High Priest," were a religious and political movement within ancient Judaism.)

The scribe asked this question of Jesus: "Which commandment is the first of all?" Jesus answered:

> *The first is…you shall love the Lord your God with all your heart, and with all your soul and with all your mind, and with all your strength (Mark 12:28-30).*

If you seek God and let Him find you in a new and transforming relationship, your love for God will be a constant in your life, a constant by which you are guided, comforted, and known.

Know this—as you change your thinking, accepting God's love and forgiveness, loving and forgiving yourself as God loves and forgives you, loving others as God loves you—you will serve God. You will come to think of yourself as a man or woman of God and you will feel the power of that relationship. Your love of God will be plain to all who come in contact with you. People will know you by who you are and what you do and they will be changed. (See Matthew 7:20.)

Rethinking and Re-ordering Your Priorities

You will know them by their fruits. (Matthew 7:20).You will know who they are by what they do.

A man in hospice lay dying, his life soon to be cut short by a terminal illness. In his lifetime, he had worked hard, formed five successful companies, two traded on the NY stock exchange. He had been successful financially, though the 2007-08 market drop and the burst of the "real estate bubble" that year had taken much of his financial wealth. He had a wife, three daughters, and one son who, due to the press of their husband's/father's business over the years, hadn't seen much of their husband and father. Over the fifty-three years of his life, the man had spent very little time with his family. On his death bed, the man was asked if he had any regrets. The question came from the dying man's son. Suffice to say, the man did *not* respond that he wished he had spent more time at the office.

This section of chapter three is about priorities—and reordering them. Discovering and embracing the power of the service driven life requires the courage of rigorous honesty—an honest look at your own life, and its fabric, its spiritual center. This may seem like a difficult and frightening task. But fear not! Having made progress in changing your thinking in the first section of this chapter, reordering your priorities becomes not only easier; it takes on now a natural and "right" feel. The place you were meant to be.

The reordering of priorities may appear an impossible task. If so, consider each of the following ideas.

Avoid "default" priorities

Something given or meriting attention before a competing alternative is a priority—something superior in rank, something more "important" than the competing alternative. Many of us have, over the years, lived with "false" priorities. Not that we were dishonest or deliberate in the ranking of our priorities. Rather, the daily demands of living—or more to the point the *perceived* daily demands of living—led us to having our priorities determined for us. We found ourselves in the middle of what felt like a life determined for us by others or by circumstances—or, worse, by some hostile force totally beyond our control. As a result, we developed resentments played out in our lives daily, often played out with those we claimed to love most.

What is essential to realize is that you *can* have control over your priorities, over the things that you make important in your life. The truth is that most of us arrive at our priorities by default, without much thought or prayer or even attention. Changing your priorities requires a deliberate act. And the good news? This deliberate act is now within your control.

Wayne Dyer[li] tells us that the energy we focus on is what we bring into our lives. When we focus, for example, on a middle school mentoring and tutoring program for kids who are at risk for failure, we bring into our lives the triumph of a child at risk for failure graduating with honors…becoming a child who is not at risk, but a child who is filled with promise. The child's mentor, a busy professional named Bruce, receives a carefully crafted gift—a piece of artwork from the child of promise graduating with honors together with a card: "For Bruce Almighty. Thank you!" ("Bruce Almighty,"[lii] a fond and fun reference to a movie by that name.) The mentors and the tutors in such programs become active participants in the miracles that happen daily. Busy people serve in this way! People who are lawyers, doctors, engineers, professionals, and businessmen and businesswomen find the time to bring love and compassion into their own lives. In doing so, they find the meaning, power and joy of a service driven life.

The mentors and tutors in such programs are busy people just like you. They are people who've learned to ask themselves the right questions:

- How do I spend my time?
- What energy do I focus upon, thereby bringing that energy into my life?
- What message am I sending to my children and to the world about what is truly important?
- Am I more interested in tutoring a child at risk or watching television?
- How can I arrange my work schedule so I can get there and back every week?

The re-ordering of your priorities does not mean doing more

The re-ordering of your priorities does not mean doing more, it means thinking differently and then doing differently.

Let's start with our thinking. For many, the ordering of priorities is often a product of very old and very unproductive thinking. Let's pinpoint what I mean by "unproductive thinking":

How much of our time is spent in worry?

How much of our time is spent in thinking about what we "can't do?"

How much of our time is spent in wondering what life would be like "if only…" If only… I had more money, if only I had a better job, if only I had more time, if only my spouse were different, if only my ex-spouse were different, if only everybody else did things the way I do things.

How much of our time is spent in negative and controlling thinking?

I want to encourage you to answer these questions honestly and consider the questions at the end of this chapter. Write down a few thoughts in this book. Pray. And then, watch out as your priorities change!

Start by doing what is necessary, and then do what is possible

If you start off by doing what is necessary and then do what is possible, you may find yourself suddenly doing the impossible!

> *[You] can do all things through Christ which strengthens [you]*
> *(Philippians 4:13).*

Pause on that beautiful piece of scripture. Don't glide over it. Rest in it for a moment. Your relationship with God is alive and active right now and it can be a source of great strength and power for you, especially if you are willing to listen to God.

St. Francis of Assisi offered more specific and practical counsel: "Start by doing what is necessary, then do what is possible, and suddenly you are doing the impossible." What does this mean for you? Do what is necessary. Perhaps that's simply reading or re-reading this chapter and considering the section below on "implementing the ideas in this chapter." Perhaps it includes writing and praying about the questions there.

Having done that, do what is possible. Perhaps a small step. Have a meal with those you love most dearly. Sit down with your children and truly talk with them—today. Do it again tomorrow. Plant a shade tree or two, literally or figuratively—today.

Think about getting out of yourself and truly emptying yourself of ego. The opportunities are many. A small sampling of service opportunities is available in Appendix 2. I hope you'll spend a few minutes perusing those pages and prayerfully considering where you feel called to serve.

As you begin to re-order perhaps decades of negative and controlling thinking, this honest look at your priorities will feel right and empowering. Your new thinking will move you head-long to new energy, passion, and joy as you begin truly to see and feel love and compassion in your life. It's exhilarating to find that *what you do every day in every part of your life is a means of service.* By finding a means to serve others, including your family, you will begin to experience true empowerment—the power of a service driven life.

As love and compassion for yourself and for others grow and your priorities change, you will begin to look for and genuinely want opportunities for service. Opportunities can be found anywhere, everywhere—at home, in business, in volunteerism. Perhaps you will be led to a service organization, like Rotary—which, in my opinion, is the most accomplished *service* organization on the face of the planet.

Ask these questions and answer them honestly:

- How am I of service?

- How can I be of service?

With God's help, re-order your priorities. chapter two speaks about seeking God and letting Him find you in prayer. Now, through prayer, let Him help you and guide you in re-ordering your priorities. He *will* help you (Isaiah 41:13; Isaiah 40:31; Psalm 121:1-2, 5; Psalm 40:1, 11, 17) and He *will* guide you (Psalm 23:1-3; Revelation 3:20). You are assured that your prayers are both "powerful" and "effective." (See James 5:16.)

Be patient with yourself. These are big changes. Many of us have spent most of our lives in unproductive thinking and default priorities—many of us have spent our lives fighting against life, not striving to align ourselves with it. Many of us have spent our lives seeking not God's will, but our own.

As your thinking and priorities change, you will discover the power of the service driven life.

"And suddenly you are doing the impossible." —St. Francis of Assisi[liii]

Stories of Service

Janet and the Food Drive

Janet joined a food and toy drive in her rural home town. She recruited nine volunteers. A child in her town opened a Christmas gift she otherwise would not. A child who otherwise would go hungry took a holiday meal with her family. In just one town, just 10 volunteers rallied together 140 boxes of food, 140 boxes of toys, and gave one of each for 140 families averaging 4 family members each; 140 x 4 lives changed! In a matter of two years, the program became a model for other food and toy drives in other towns, in other states, in other countries, around the globe.

It's a great story, don't you think? Janet's work reminds me of the old Methodist hymn, "There's a Spirit in the Air":

> *"When a hungry child is fed, praise the love that Christ revealed;*
>
> *living, working, in our world."*[liv]

However, you may be surprised at what Janet thought about her work. Let's rewind the story and hear it told by Janet in her own words[lv]:

"I believed I was nothing, worthless. My head told me exactly that and, boy, did I believe it for years—no, for decades. In my 30's, I was divorced, childless, feeling caught in a job I hated. Caught in an existence without meaning. I was severely depressed and sometimes suicidal.

"One day, I was invited to participate in a food and toy drive for a local charity. The same invitation had been given me several years running. I had consistently said 'no.' For some reason, this time, I said 'yes.' And I got to work, recruiting volunteers and organizing. We served many families.

"I saw tears in the eyes of those we served; I saw humility, gratefulness, joy in families in my own town—my own state and country—who did not know from where the next food was coming. After the drive was over, I realized that I had seen something else. I had seen God in the eyes of those I served... and suddenly I knew it. It scared me at first, but it also gave me the quiet comfort of God moving in my life. In *my* life! Extraordinary! I was driven to agree to chair the next drive and to grow the project.

"Over time, with God's help and in His presence, I began to learn love and compassion—*for me!* I began to learn that I am God's creation and that I am good. As I learned, and as my thinking changed, I found myself alive with love and compassion for others. There is no greater gift."

Henry the Trial Lawyer[lvi]

Love [others] as I have loved you (John 15:12; also John 13:34-35).

I'd like to share with you a story about new priorities and a true "do over."

To everyone who knew him, Henry was a very successful lawyer. In truth, he hated his job, but he worked hard at it anyway and it consumed his time and energies. He worked constantly and was known as an excellent litigator—a trial lawyer willing and able to "take down almost anybody." Henry and his wife had one daughter, Jessica, 10 years old. His daughter attended a private boarding school 200 miles from the family home.

One late night, on the way home from the office, Henry stopped at a convenience store to pick up some cigarettes. As he was leaving the store, a young man with a gun held up the convenience store. In the chaos that ensued, Henry was shot in the head. Henry was gravely wounded, but survived the gunshot. Because of the damage to his brain, Henry was forced to learn all over again how to speak and how to think. After nearly a year of painful and painstaking rehabilitation, Henry returned to work.

Henry still hated his job, but something had changed inside of Henry. He began to explore other vocations and eventually, he stopped practicing law. One day in the fall, he left the office for the last time, went home to pick up his daughter's beloved dog, and drove 200 miles to his daughter's boarding school. He and the dog found Jessica in a school assembly, where the school's Head Mistress was addressing the student body. Henry and Jessica, both in tears, hugged, while the dog jumped for joy on his two hind legs. "Henry," said the head mistress, "we're in a session here."

"I'm sorry to interrupt," said Henry, "but I've missed my daughter's first eleven years...I don't want to miss any more."

Henry and his daughter (and her best friend) went home together where they met up with Henry's wife, Jessica's mother. That night, for the first time in years, they all shared a meal together. Henry never returned to the practice of law and Jessica never returned to the boarding school.

Henry's story is in some ways unique. Henry's priorities were in a sense re-ordered by a gunshot wound to the head. Through his experience, Henry re-ordered his priorities—he found a new vocation he loved, a vocation rewarding in every way.

Through his change in priorities, Henry found a huge release of love and compassion for his child and his spouse. He began to serve through home and family. Does this mean that you must quit your job to serve home and family? Of course not. Vocation is itself one of the ways we serve our families. And thankfully, it does not require a gunshot wound to change and re-order priorities—or our thinking.

What I hope you see in Henry's story is that Henry came to know that he needed a drastic re-ordering of priorities and a new definition of "success." And he acted upon that. He came to know the truest and purest form of service—boundless love in his own home. In changing your priorities, act deliberately. Answer honestly the questions that follow this chapter. Ask for, and receive, God's help. Take action. Now.

Implementing the Ideas in This chapter

Please note that the focus points at the end of this chapter are divided into two parts—one on changing our thinking and the other on changing our priorities. Take your time as you peruse this part of the book. This section provides a reflective pause for you to consider what God is saying to you through this chapter.

Focus on Scripture/Change Your Thinking

I am not ashamed of the Gospel. It is the power of God... (Romans 1:16).

I am a source of goodness...of love and compassion and forgiveness, serenity, and peace. I am imperfect, but I am God's creation. I am created in His image (Genesis 1:27-28) and I am therefore good (Genesis 1:31) and filled with the capacity to love.

Focus on Scripture/Change Your Priorities

You will know them by their fruits. (Matthew 7:20) You will know who they are by what they do.

Immediately they left their nets and followed Him (Matthew 4:18-22).

Chapter Review/Change Your Thinking

Focus on these specific ways—covered in this chapter—to change your thinking. If you think it would be helpful, return to each of these topics in the chapter.

- How do I think of myself?
- Accept and embrace God's unconditional love, forgiveness, redemption
- Love and forgive yourself as God loves and forgives you
- Freed to love and forgive others as God loves and forgives you
- Love God; think of yourself as a man or woman of God

Chapter Review/Change Your Priorities

Focus on these specific ways—covered in this chapter—to change your thinking. If you think it would be helpful, return to each of these topics in the chapter.

- Avoid default priorities
- Re-ordering your priorities does not mean doing more; it means thinking differently and then doing differently.
- Start by doing what is necessary, then do what is possible, and suddenly you're doing the impossible.

Questions to Write and Pray About/Change Your Thinking

What about my thinking do I need to change, would I like to change?

_____

_____

_____

Can I acknowledge that changing my thinking is about me, and that if I ask for help God will help and comfort me?

_____

_____

_____

What about my thinking holds me back from who I really want to be and what I really want to do?

_____

_____

_____

Do I see myself as a source of goodness…of love and compassion and forgiveness?

_____

_____

_____

Am I truly able to love myself and thereby begin a "lifelong romance?"

_____

_____

_____

Do I treat myself with love and compassion?

_____

_____

_____

Is that love and compassion reflected in what I do and how I am—at home, at work, in my life, and in the lives of those I touch?

_____

_____

_____

Can I truly embrace love and compassion—for myself first, and for others?

_____

_____

_____

Do I see myself as a man or woman of God?

_____

_____

_____

If not, what do I need to do to see myself that way?

_____

_____

_____

Questions to Write and Pray About/Change Your Priorities

What are my priorities now, today?

_____

_____

_____

How am I of service?

_____

_____

_____

What do my priorities say about me?

_____

_____

How did I feel, and what did I think about, when I read Henry's story?

_____

_____

_____

What have I missed in my life and the lives of those I love as a result of my thinking and my priorities?

_____

_____

_____

How much of my time is spent thinking about what I cannot do?

_____

_____

_____

How much "if only…" thinking do I do?

_____

_____

_____

How much of my time is spent in negative and controlling thinking?

_____

_____

_____

How does my thinking affect my priorities?

_____

_____

_____

What energy am I focusing on, and thus bringing into my life?

_____

_____

_____

What would it be like to get out of myself, even for a moment, and truly empty myself of ego?

_____

_____

_____

What are the things in my life that have brought me, and bring me, energy, passion, and joy?

_____

_____

_____

How can I be of service?

_____

_____

_____

Chapter 4

Discover the Joy in the Service Driven Life

*"I have said these things to you
so that My joy may be in you and that
your joy may be complete."*

–John 15:11

The story is told of a man who was constantly unhappy. But more than that, he was always restless, filled with discontent, constantly dissatisfied with his place in life, both physically and emotionally. This haunting place was filled with almost constant foreboding about where he was at the moment and what the future would hold. The man constantly felt that he wasn't physically where he was supposed to be and certainly "knew" that he wasn't emotionally where he should be. If he was at home, he felt he should be at the gym. If at work, he felt he should be at home. If he was anywhere at all, surely he should be elsewhere—perhaps some other place he didn't even know about. Uneasiness was his constant companion and a confusion, a total lack of peace, wracked him daily. He was a permanent resident of a very dark place, a place where things never seemed quite "as they should be."

If you've ever been in such a place, I have wonderful news. As you draw close to God and let Him find you, He will help you to change your thinking about yourself and your priorities. You will begin to feel a huge change in yourself; you will experience a new peace, a true contentment and a knowing that where you are—physically and emotionally—is exactly where you are supposed to be and that "all is well." Whether you are sitting at your desk, working out, grocery shopping, or walking on a beautiful wilderness trail, it just feels right. "All is well." For many, that feeling (even in small doses) is brand new. Does that mean that you will always be pleased with the place you are and the things that are happening and the feelings you are having at the moment? Probably not. Does that mean that you will never need to change the "place" you are, emotionally or physically? Of course not.

What it does mean is that you are now on a path of great meaning and power and joy, a path upon which you are accompanied by a God of love and compassion—a present God "from whence cometh your help." God is good! He will accompany you and delight in you as a man or woman of goodness, capable of great love, compassion, and forgiveness. And what joy there is in that!

As we travel the path toward meaning and power, toward the service driven life, we find ourselves becoming fully alive. C. S. Lewis wrote that we live in the "shadowlands." "The sun is always shining somewhere else—around the bend in the road, over the brow of the hill."[lvii] No, it is not! It is shining right now, on you, in your life, where you are now!

Your Joy Is in God

In a fundamental way, the joy in the service driven life is rooted in and emanates from your decision to seek God and let Him find you. You have sought a new and intimate and loving relationship with God. And He has found you. In that alone, there is great joy! Both Old and New Testaments of the Bible are filled with references to the joy found in a relationship with God. Here are some incredible psalms of joy:

> Then I will go to… God, to God my exceeding joy (Psalm 43:4).

> Our mouths were filled with laughter. Our tongues with shouts of joy.
> The Lord has done great things, and we rejoice (Psalm 126:2-3).

Psalm 16 is called a "miktam" (the Hebrew word) of David, a song of trust and confidence in God:

> You show me the path of life. In your presence there is fullness of joy!
> (Psalm 16:11).

And finally, from the prophet Isaiah:

> …everyone who thirsts, come to the waters…. For you shall go out in
> joy, and be led forth in peace; the mountains and the hills before you
> shall burst into song, and all the trees of the field shall clap their hands
> (Isaiah 55:1,12 RSV).

From the apostle Paul, in his letter to the Roman congregations:

> The God of hope fills you with His joy and peace in believing, so that you
> may abound in hope by the power of the Holy Spirit (Romans 15:13).

> …for the joy of the Lord is your strength (Nehemiah 8:10).

"Can you not feel the joy of knowing, loving and companying with God?"[lviii] Pause now and feel the joy in these words. Knowing, loving, and companying with a God of love, forgiveness, compassion and redemption, a God of help and guidance and comfort, a God of nearness and inseparability —present, now and always.

Focus especially on the word "companying." This word and its usage comes from the April 18 meditation of God Calling. As I mentioned earlier, the two authors of God Calling declined to take credit for the writing of the book. They remained and remain anonymous, in part because they believe to their core that the words in their book are not theirs—they are God's. If you spend any significant time with the book *God Calling*, it is difficult not to see God moving and speaking in these meditations. In many cases, the words used are antiquated, an unusual usage for our modern age, and yet they seem to be the perfect words! The use of "companying" is just such a word.

In the April 18 meditation, you are asked to "…feel the joy of… companying with God." What a truly wonderful and, indeed joyful, usage. "Companying" is a transitive verb. That is, an action verb with a "direct object." In this usage, the action verb is "companying" and the direct object is God. Think about this phrase as describing a great change in your relationship with God—a word which describes you taking action, seeking Him. He has found you and now you are "companying" with God and He with you. And what does it mean to "company" with God? It means nothing short of being *with* God, accompanying an ever-present God. This one word and its usage calls attention to a relationship both intimate and joyful. If you learn to company with God, you simply cannot be alone. It's that simple. Joy without measure—joy in God.

And when sorrow comes, as it will and it does, the thirtieth psalm reminds us that while sorrow may endure for a night, "joy cometh in the morning." Yes, sorrow may come. But consider this—joy can now be a constant in your life, if you allow it to be! Even in the midst of great sorrow and difficulty, you can learn to "…anticipate the morning and feel in the night of sorrow that underlying joy that tells of confident expectations of the morning."[lix] That underlying joy is found in God.

Your Joy Is in Service

One of the ways we "company" with God is in service. God gives us the commandment—nay, the gift—of service, and therein lies great joy. That joy is built in and God-given. It is joy for those who are served and great joy for those who serve. Albert Einstein, a man with multiple layers of genius, was once asked this question: Who among us makes the greatest and most meaningful contribution to humanity? His answer: "He who brings out of love a cup of water to a thirsty man."[lx]

Water is essential for life. The obvious benefit for the man who receives the cup is easy to grasp. But the amazing, and in some ways even more important, part of the story is found in what comes to the one who *brings* the cup. That person is the true beneficiary. The giver is the one who finds meaning and purpose, energy, and passion, and discovers that, in service, there is great joy.

In 1987, a service club makes a commitment to eradicate the wild polio virus from the face of the planet. What followed were 2.2 billion polio vaccines in eighteen years—most administered in third world countries by volunteers—a 99 percent drop in new polio cases. Today, as the world stands on the brink of the eradication of polio, and as you read this book, an estimated seven million children walk the planet crutch-free, indeed polio-free, because those volunteers were there, and only because those volunteers were there.

A friend of mine has a prominent post on her Facebook page. The post is always there, never changes. It is a constant. "I will always remember the two little girls I *got to* immunize in West Bengal, India. That experience, and one little boy with polio, changed me and changed my life forever."

The miraculous part of the story of polio eradication is two-fold. There is the obvious meaning of the vaccine to those immunized against this horrific and much-feared disease. But there is incredible meaning that comes to those who are servants in this life-changing and life-saving program. These servants administered life-changing vaccines in third-world countries around the globe—servants driven to find meaning and purpose outside of themselves, passion and hope, and great joy, within. Allow me to share the words of my Facebook friend,[lxi] one of these servants:

> *I am not a doctor. I am just a volunteer who has learned to administer the life-savings drops of the oral polio vaccine. I stood in a small lean-to home in a village in India, with a mother and her three children. One of the children, a young boy, already had polio. As I began to administer the oral polio vaccine to the two children without polio, I noticed out of the corner of my eye the young boy, his legs crippled over by the disease, as he shuffled on his knees across the matted dirt floor of the house. I thought of the volunteer medical doctors already at work in the same village, providing help to children for whom the vaccine came too late—children with paralytic polio receiving respiratory monitoring and support, physical therapy, leg braces, even orthopedic surgery. Help and care and support for victims of a devastating disease for which there is no cure.*

I finished the vaccinations and looked at the mother. She was weeping. Through an interpreter, I asked about the tears. Said the mother: "I've cried myself to sleep about my son's polio. I am cried out. So I give it to God as best I can. These tears," she pointed to her face, "these tears are tears of joy that two of my children will never experience such agony and horror." The mother thanked me for coming and told me that I must be an angel from God. At that moment in my life, I felt a joy I had never felt before. Ever.

And then there is the story of Peter.[lxii] Peter was a real estate broker who was a Rotarian, a member of a local Rotary Club. Every Thursday afternoon, Peter participated in a Rotary-sponsored middle school mentoring and tutoring program for kids at risk. Every week, Peter was at the school where he mentored two students. These students were very much at-risk and in need.

One day, Peter came to me and told me that he was going through a work-related transition and was having some financial difficulties and could no longer be a Rotarian. With a tear in his eye, Peter continued, "May I continue to mentor and tutor, even though I'm not a Rotarian?"

"Yes, you bet," I said. "That's what the kids need. You're a great asset to the program. And besides, we tutors and mentors will get to see you regularly, too."

"Thank you," said Peter. And he started to leave the room. I hesitated.

"Peter," I called out as he reached the door, "you've got a lot on your plate right now. You can take a break if you need to."

Peter paused, turned around—the tear in his eye was now on his cheek—and said simply: "No, I need this. It is a place of great joy in my life." Indeed.

Yes, in service there is great joy, built in. There is joy for those served and great joy for those who serve. Love and compassion and joy abide. But there is more!

Your Complete Joy Is in God and Service

As we truly embrace the servant's heart, we find the meaning and the power that accompanies those who live in service. We revel in the comfort of God's presence, in His guidance, in the knowledge we are not alone—and we find ourselves living with great joy, moving toward a complete joy found *only* in His service.

We have sought God and He has found us. We have found comfort and joy in the knowledge that God stands at the door and knocks, that He draws near and abides with us, and that His voice can be heard, now and always. We have examined the powerful connection between God and service and re-ordered our thinking and our priorities. We have found a way to live in love, compassion, and forgiveness—for ourselves and for others. The power of these steps in the journey cannot be overstated.

Now, we make certain that we have truly opened the door to God's knock and that we have let Him in and have supped with Him. We have learned that it is in love, compassion, and forgiveness for ourselves and others that we truly serve God. Now, we are led to serve Him by serving others—with constancy, with energy and passion, with purpose, and with joy beyond measure.

Not only are we led to serve Him by serving others; indeed, we are commanded to serve Him by serving others. If you find the word "commandment" to be "off putting" (in the old English usage), you are not alone. But hear this: the word "commandment"—a word which once may have suggested rigid rules and orders—now brings to you a life-changing invitation to power and meaning in your life. This commandment is actually an invitation to a place of great joy, of complete joy. In the upper room, as Jesus prepared to "go to Him who sent me" (John 16:5), Jesus told the disciples this:

> *This is My commandment, that you love one another as I have loved you (John 15:12).*

> *If you keep My commandment, you will abide in my love. I have said these things to you so that My joy may be in you and that your joy may be complete (John 15:10-11).*

That your joy may be *complete!*

Pause now, and think about these words of scripture. Revel in them, be comforted by them. Joy "cometh" not in the morning; joy cometh *now!* In *complete* joy we find ourselves in hope and purpose and passion, resting in His arms, resting in love and compassion for ourselves and others, and companying with God on our path of service. We can be secure in the knowledge that what we do for ourselves dies with us, but what we do for others is and remains truly immortal.

I hope you will spend some time now with the stories of service that follow this chapter. In these stories, there is meaning, power *and great joy*. And there is God. You can feel Him near as you read about the lives of those served and, most important, as you read about the lives of those who serve.

Stories of Service

This is my commandment that you love one another as I have loved you (John 15:12.). If you keep My commandment, you will abide in My love. I have said these things to you so that My joy may be in you and that your joy may be complete (John 15:10-11).

Josh and the Mentor

Josh lived with his grandmother, a woman who struggled with active alcoholism. No parent anywhere to be found. Before his introduction to a mentor and tutor, Josh was truly programmed for failure not just in middle school, but in life. However, with the help of a Rotary mentor and tutor, a professional man, Josh turned it around and graduated high school and went on to college.

At age seventeen, Josh wrote down some thoughts about the impact of what he had been through in a letter to his mentor:[lxiii]

> *To my mentor and tutor,*
>
> *When you thought I wasn't looking, I saw you frame my first attempt at drawing and I immediately wanted to draw another.*
>
> *When you thought I wasn't looking, I saw you bring pizza to our middle school, expecting nothing in return, and I learned those little things can be the special things in life.*
>
> *When you thought I wasn't looking, I heard you say a prayer and I knew there is a God I could always talk to and I learned to trust in God.*
>
> *When you thought I wasn't looking, I saw you send a card to a friend who was sick, and I learned that we all have to help take care of each other.*
>
> *When you thought I wasn't looking, I saw you give of your time and money to help people who had nothing and I learned that those who have something should give to those who don't.*

When you thought I wasn't looking, I saw you take care of your home and everyone in it, and I learned we have to take care of what we are given.

When you thought I wasn't looking, I saw how you handled your responsibilities even when you didn't feel good, and I learned that I would have to be responsible when I grow up.

When you thought I wasn't looking, I saw tears in your eyes, and I learned that sometimes things hurt, but it's all right to cry.

When you thought I wasn't looking, I saw that you cared and I wanted to be everything I could be.

When you thought I wasn't looking, I learned most of life's lessons that I need to be a good person when I grow up.

When you thought I wasn't looking, I looked at you and wanted to say: "Thanks, for all the things I saw when you thought I wasn't looking."

This young man's life was turned around by one man in service, through the power of service in a service driven life. Josh's mentor writes:[lxiv]

I, the mentor, am blessed to have found this program. Through this program, I have learned a lot. One day, early in my mentoring, I was sitting with Josh. We were working on physics, of all things. I felt fairly useless, since I was not highly trained in the sciences. I was working as hard as Josh at figuring out the problem posed in the textbook. We worked it out together; it was a victory. After Josh left for the day, I couldn't seem to get up and leave. I sat there in a small middle school classroom, all alone—at least, I thought I was alone. At that moment, I felt something brand new inside me. I felt led. I felt guided. I felt I had help in what I was doing—not just in the physics problem, but in my service to Josh and other kids in the program. I felt excited. I felt within me a joy I had never experienced.

I had never been a man of faith. I had never thought of myself as spiritual. I had never thought of myself as a servant, with a servant *heart. But that fall day, I learned more than the solution to a physics problem. I learned that God moves in my life; in **my** life! I learned that He is present with me and I felt at that moment His presence. And when I read what Josh wrote to me years later, I knew beyond all doubt that God had led me and helped me.*

*This tutoring and mentoring program has changed me. I get to watch Josh's extraordinary achievement; I have a lifelong friend. And I have learned that I can never be alone. Immanuel; God with me. Can there be any doubt that through my service, **I** am changed? And that my joy is complete?*

Kevin's Mentor

Kevin lived with his mother in a single parent family. At the time he entered the 7th Inning Stretch Program, a middle school mentoring and tutoring program of the Sunrise Rotary Club of San Clemente, California, Kevin had no positive male presence in the home and there was no real parenting going on.

Kevin entered the 7thInning Stretch mentoring and tutoring program as a "D" and "F" student. Although English is his primary language, he was virtually unable to speak—or wouldn't speak—at school. Kevin was truly unable to cope with school. He had high absenteeism, low reading skills, frequent disciplinary problems and, even in middle school, a tendency toward gang activity.

In the fall of 1995, Kevin entered the program and began slowly working with his tutor. He participated, quietly at first, in mentoring events. In time, something began to change. Kevin began to speak to his tutor—to ask a question. He grew to accept help in getting organized and even talked about what he was interested in, about what might be his passion in career. He listened to his mentor when he explained why this whole "school thing" mattered. And finally, the best part of all, a smile.

Within two and a half school quarters, Kevin went from "D" and "F" student to "A" student, not only coping, but excelling. He went on to become the program's Student of the Year that year. He and his mom attended the end of year Rotary Presidential celebration that year and a young man who, at entry into the program, was unable to speak at school, spoke eloquently to ninety Rotarians and spouses about his experience in the 7th Inning Stretch and the impact of Rotary in his life.

Kevin's mother was moved enough to declare a new intention to improve her parenting.

Five years later, Kevin went on to graduate high school with honors and attended Princeton University on a full academic scholarship. He will soon be a physician.

Kevin's tutor/mentor[lxv] says, "Kevin no longer needs a tutor. I am honored to say that I am still his mentor. I am honored, changed, renewed, and joyful."

Kevin's mentor served God by serving others.

The Joy of Peer Mentoring

Rotary Youth Leadership Awards (RYLA) is set up so that Rotarians work together with youth in leadership development, but it is also about youth working with youth. In the end, RYLA encourages peers to mentor other kids. Brennan Clinebell, my son, attended RYLA during his junior year of high school and returned to RYLA as an alumnus in his senior year:[lxvi]

> My name is Brennan Clinebell. I love God; I love music and sports and have a passion for service. I am driven by my community and inspired by those around me to make this world better. The reason that I returned to RYLA in my senior year was to give back and to spread the lessons that it teaches to people at my school and my community. I love the thought of turning every high school into a "RYLA High." RYLA showed me that it's okay to be myself and be proud of it. RYLA opened me up to new people and brought me out of my shell. I am so excited to show this year's kids the joys and opportunities that RYLA offers. Thank you!

As I read these lines written by Brennan, I think of Isaiah 55:12 which says, *For you shall go out in joy, and be led back in peace; the mountains and the hills before you shall burst into song, and all the trees of the field shall clap their hands* (Isaiah 55:12). Amen!

73

Implementing the Ideas in This chapter

Focus on Scripture

I have said these things to you so that My joy may be in you and that your joy may be complete (John 15:11).

For you shall go out in joy (Isaiah 55:12)...

You show me the path of life. In your presence there is fullness of joy. (Psalm 16:11).

... for the joy of the Lord is your strength (Nehemiah 8:10).

(See also Psalm 43:4; Romans 15:13).

Chapter Review

Focus on these specific ways, covered in this chapter, to find the joy in the service driven life. If you think it would be helpful, return to each of these topics in the chapter.

- Your joy is in God.
- Your joy is in service.
- Your complete joy is in God and service.

Questions to Write and Pray About

How would it feel to me to serve God by serving others?

_____

_____

_____

Can I be open to God working in my life and the lives of others?

_____

_____

_____

Can I be open to God's guidance in serving others?

_____

_____

_____

Can I truly embrace love and compassion—for myself and for others?

_____

_____

_____

Have I experienced joy in my relationship with God? If so, when? If not, how would that feel?

_____

_____

_____

Have I experienced joy in service? If so, when? If not, how would that feel?

_____

_____

_____

Have I ever experienced "complete joy" as described in John 15:9-12?

_____

_____

_____

Can I truly embrace the flood of energy and passion and joy which results when I truly embrace my servant heart?

_____

_____

_____

Chapter 5

Discover Your Path of Service

You will know them by their fruits. (Matthew 7:16).
You will know who they are by what they do.

"What good amid these, O me! O life?
Answer: That you are here—that life exists and identity.
That the the powerful play goes on
and you may contribute a verse."
—Walt Whitman[xvii]

You show me the path of life.

In your presence there is fullness of joy.
(Psalms 16:11; Acts 2:28).

In this chapter, you can find specific direction about *your* path, *your* verse. What will your verse be? As I write this, I am excited for you and for those you will serve, through home and family, through vocation, and through neighbor. It is time truly to discover your path of service. Remember, you are not alone on this journey. You are *never* alone. God is ever present on your journey, on your path—ever a source of strength and help. Embrace now the service driven life in every part of your life—through home and family, through vocation, and through neighbor.

Serve Through Home and Family

As we've seen, the first mission field is home and family. We are commanded to love others as God loves us. "And where does this love begin? In our own home."[lxviii] The truest and purest act of service is in loving another unconditionally. That truth will nowhere be more visible and fulfilling than in the love and compassion released at home, in a deep and rich passion and joy. Embrace it! Strive to embrace fully the flow of love and compassion for your spouse, for your children, and for other human souls. What you do in your home and in your family can now be the truest and purest form of service, bringing love and compassion and forgiveness and joy to all in your home. Here are some ways to help you embrace the truest form of service.

1. Words Can Love, Words Can Hurt

What you say matters.

> *Death and life are in the power of the tongue (Proverbs 18:21).*

> *How great a forest is set ablaze by a small fire. And the tongue is a fire (James 3:5-6).*

James chapter three goes on to say that no one can tame the tongue. With our tongue we can bless the Lord and Father, yet with the same tongue we "curse those who are made in the likeness of God" (vs. 9). And when this scripture says "those who are made in the likeness of God," that includes every living soul.

If we continue in the book of James, we find a warning against judging others. A judgment that begins in our thoughts often finds its way to our mouths.

Whoever judges another, speaks evil against the law and judges the law,
is a judge. There is one lawgiver and one judge... (James 4:11-12).

That one lawgiver and one judge is God. In the first book of the New Testament, Jesus gives a similar admonition against judging others. Let's look at His words here:

Do not judge, so that you may not be judged. For with the judgment
you make you will be judged, and the measure you give will be the
measure you get. Why do you see the speck in your brother's eye (some
translations say 'neighbor's eye'), but do not notice the log in your own
eye? Or how can you say to your brother, 'Let me take the speck out
of your eye,' while the log is in your own eye. First take the log out of
your own eye, and then you will see clearly to take the speck out of your
brother's eye (Matthew 7:1-5).

Does all of this mean there is never judgment on this earth? Of course not. Our legal system metes out judgment all the time and not just judgment for evildoers. In the words of one commentator, the admonition against judging others "...does not exclude ethical awareness."

Does all of this mean that we will never "judge" another in our lives? No, we are not perfect. But it certainly means we strive with all of our strength and all of our faith not to judge those we love most dearly. We are here to love, not judge those most precious to us, with whom we share home and family. These are the individuals with whom we want to have honesty, openness, and true intimacy. We strive with all of our strength and faith to give to those we love unconditional acceptance and unconditional love as we have received from God. "God is love...no judging. God is love... no resentment. God is love...all patience."[lxix] The image of the speck and the "log" in Matthew 7 suggests to us that if we first take the log out of our own eye, we can then speak to those we love with a new understanding and compassion.

Matthew chapters 5-7 include a series of Jesus' teachings. Matthew 5:1-2 describes how Jesus "went up the mountain; and after he sat down, His disciples came to Him. Then he began to speak, and taught them..." It is in these passages that we find the teachings of Jesus concerning prayer (the Lord's prayer), the Beatitudes, doing to others as you would have them do to you and the admonition against judging others. Toward the end of chapter 7, at

Matthew 7:24-25, Jesus tells the disciples that those who hear His teachings and act upon them will be like a wise man who built his house on rock:

> *The rain fell, the floods came, and the winds blew and beat on that house, but it did not fall, because it had been founded on rock.*

The disciples were astounded at the great wisdom of His teaching, teaching that was given not as a scribe but as from one of authority (Matthew 7:28).

Found your home on rock, not sand (Matthew 7:24-27). Think about what you say out loud in your home and to those you love most dearly.

Is this your tongue?

"I love and cherish you."

"I am grateful for who you are."

"I love supporting you in every way, emotionally and financially."

Or is your tongue an instrument of "fire" that sets ablaze a "great fire"?

And how can you know for sure that your words are loving and not hurtful? Anyone who has heard a preacher preach is likely to have heard the words of Psalm 19:14. But this oft-quoted psalm is much more than a preface to the words of a preacher. Consider it more carefully:

> *Let the words of my mouth and the meditation of my heart be acceptable to You, O Lord, my rock and my redeemer (Psalm 19:14).*

These words of the psalmist counsel us to ask for help and to teach us to pray that our words and thoughts will be acceptable to God. And just what is acceptable? What is acceptable before God is love and forgiveness, as God has loved and forgiven us. He wants nothing less than the two greatest commandments:

> *Love God with all your heart, soul, mind and strength; and love one another as I have loved you (John 13:34-35; Mark 12:28-31).*

Remember, what we say matters. You may have heard children say, "Sticks and stones will break my bones but words can never hurt me." As adults, I think we all know that the notion that "words cannot hurt" is fundamentally false. Words hurt. Ask a psychotherapist or psychiatrist engaged in marriage counseling how often he or she hears from a client about something hurtful the client's spouse said to them. Or ask a child therapist about hurtful words from parent to child. Such words often stay with us for years. If unaddressed, forgiveness and intimacy can become impossible. Words can set back relationships for years upon years or they can take relationships to a new and joyous level of love and compassion. Use words to bless rather than harm those you love most (James 3:1-12).

What we *don't* say matters as well. How long has it been since you spoke words of love and compassion, out loud, to those you love? Spend time considering this question—the question of how long it has been. Spend no time berating yourself if you have fallen short. Instead, act now, today, to change that.

There is another way that what you don't say matters. There are times when saying nothing is the most loving thing you can do. Are you a person who has to be "right?" When you talk with the people or person most important to you, do you need to be right? Many will sacrifice everything—serenity, peace, self, relationships—on the altar of "being right."

Try this. Just for today, try not having to be right. If you are engaged in discussion with the one you love and you think you are right and you feel compelled to tell that loved one you are right—don't. Wait an hour, wait a day, and see whether you still need to be right. See how that feels. In the meantime, say nothing—except, perhaps, "*you* [your loved one] may be right."

The purpose of such an exercise is to help you choose love and compassion and to see how that feels. Choose love and compassion. Choose humility. God opposes the proud, but gives grace to the humble. (See James 4:6.) Humble yourself before God and He will exalt you. (See James 4:10.) Humble yourself before God and use your words to prevent conflict and dispute. (See James 4:1-12.) When we use words in love and compassion, we can step aside and watch amazing things happen to the peace and serenity in our own lives, in our home, and in the relationships we value most of all in this world. Choose love and compassion, and thereby invite joy into your home.

There is another time when saying nothing is the most loving thing you can do. When you are feeling pain, hurt, or anger, what you say to those you love most must be carefully screened. Perhaps what you are tempted to say comes not from a "clean" place of honest feeling, but rather from feelings that are all about you and have nothing what-so-ever to do with those you love. In these moments, say nothing. Are you a person who tends toward sarcasm? If so, don't. Remember the origin of that word "sarcasm": from the Latin "sarcasmos" and the Greek "sarkasmos" meaning "to tear flesh." "Sharp utterance designed to cut or give pain."[lxx] Ow! Do not use your tongue to hurt others; do not "curse those who are made in the likeness of God." (See James 3:9.) When in doubt, say nothing. Go to God, return to prayer, and speak later!

Words can love. Words can hurt. You can make the choice.

2. Remember Henry.[lxxi]

Henry said, "I missed my daughter's first eleven years. I don't want to miss any more." Like Henry, what have *you* missed in your life and the lives of those you love as a result of your thinking and your priorities? Write about that. Pray about that. If you've fallen short, accept that and forgive yourself. Okay, so you've fallen short. But you are also a person who is willing to look at yourself and ask yourself some difficult questions; and you are willing to do the work to grow and progress. Were that not true, you would have put this book down long ago. Accept having fallen short, make amends where necessary, then forgive. Until you forgive yourself, you cannot and will not move forward.

Perhaps think about your life as if you've been given a new chance to live in a new and exciting way. And that is exactly what you have before you! What does that mean for you? What can be different? What can you do, with God's help, to bring love and compassion—and a little peace and serenity—to your home and to those you love most? Pray about it and let God lead you. If you open yourself up to God's help and guidance in your home, you will be well along the path to embracing the truest form of service. And you will be an instrument of His peace and His will.

3. Be a Force for Love and Forgiveness in Your Home

I mentioned earlier a wonderful little book called *God Calling*.[lxxii] Savor these words, found in the April 16 entry from that book:

> *"Dwell on My actions on earth. See in them love in operation…*
> *You too must put love (God) into action in your lives.*
>
> *Perfect love means perfect forgiveness. Lo, my children, you see that where*
> *God is there can be no lack of forgiveness, for that is really lack of love."*

Remember that where there is love and forgiveness, God is present. What a spectacular, comforting concept! When we love and forgive others as God has loved and forgiven us, joy cometh in the morning. Be a constant in times of calm, contentment, serenity, and prosperity and, perhaps more importantly, in times of pain, suffering, sorrow, addiction, loneliness, conflict. Yes, it is difficult to love and forgive in times of pain and conflict and stress. But remember, you are not alone. Ask for His help.

Ask for His help as you love and forgive yourself. You cannot practice love and forgiveness in your home without first loving and forgiving yourself. That's a tough hurdle and if you need help in this area, you can return to chapter three and work again on implementing the ideas there. The good news is that as you practice love and forgiveness for yourself and in your home, it will begin to feel like the "place" you were meant to be. And it is. You will then be a constant—not perfect, but a constant—in the modeling of the two greatest commandments: loving God with all your heart and all your soul, and loving others as God loves you. (See Mark 12:28-31; Luke 10:25-28; John 13:34-35; John 15:12; John 15:17.) I want to encourage you to begin in your home. Today.

4. "Preach the gospel and when necessary use words."

This section is titled with the words of St. Francis of Assisi,[lxxiii] spoken some eight hundred years ago. These words are still with us because they are that important! Preach the gospel in your home and when necessary, use words. This means loving through your actions those in your home, just as God has loved you. (See Luke 10:1-11.) Go where He would go and do what He would do. (See John 15:12.) As you have seen in me, do the same. (See Luke 10:1-11.

> *Little children, let us love, not in word or speech, but in truth and action (1 John 3:18).*

As we read and think about these scriptures, they have a way of becoming a part of us and enabling us actively to model their truths. We find our thoughts changed and suddenly we walk in the ability to live them out with love and joy, with home and family. Yes, we also want to do this beyond our home—but the home is the first mission field, the place where you seek to build lasting and intimate relationships with those most precious. Embrace them. Build your faith and thereby, build theirs. There is no truer and purer form of service.

Know that what you model for your children will be a part of them. What you model can be a wonderful foundation for your children's future, a model they will be attracted to and want to embrace in their own lives. Or, what you model can be for them a source of ongoing struggle and pain. Are you giving your children a chain that needs to be broken? Or are you giving them a chain that will support and protect them, and set them free? Are you giving them the gift of a life well lived—a life filled with meaning, power and joy? Are you showing them a love of God, a love of themselves, and a love of serving others? Are you daily showing them love and compassion—love and compassion for those most precious to you? If not, start now. Nothing is more important. Nothing!

5. Think Differently, Act Differently

In chapter three, I talked about changing your thinking and re-ordering your priorities. In your home, this is absolutely crucial. As you've seen, the setting of priorities is often a result of very unproductive, default thinking. "I don't have time" is not much of a justification for ignoring family—particularly if much of your time is spent in worry, in "if only" thinking. If negative and controlling thinking is currently your primary stock in trade—or worse, if you currently live in fear—know that you *can* think differently and then do differently. It takes work, but the rewards are beyond all measure.

It may help to return to chapter three and consider how your thinking and your priorities have affected your relationships at home. Remember Henry and his "do-over." Then, make a conscious decision, with God's help, not to miss another important moment in your children's lives. Make a conscious decision to listen with love and compassion to your spouse and to those most precious in your life. Make a conscious decision to hear complete sentences and thoughts from those you love—without interruption, without formulating and commencing your response in the middle of their sentences and thoughts.

Make a conscious decision to act first out of love and not out of worry or fear, a conscious decision to look at what holds you back from intimacy with the most important people in your life.

Then "do differently." Have a meal with your family. Have two meals with your family. Have another. And watch relationships grow and bloom, in good or bad times. Watch and feel the change in you—and watch as you feel what you are doing and how you are with them. Sit down with your spouse. Talk with him or her. Listen. Love. Live in gratefulness. By changing you, you can change the dynamic in your home. There is such joy in that.

And if, periodically, you find yourself busy at work, busy with other things, that's okay. When you do have time with family, fill that time with love and compassion, with love and forgiveness. Talk with those you love about your schedule. Talk about how much you miss them when other things occupy you. Talk about your love for those most precious, *to* those most precious. Nourish your relationships. However long or short the time, this is time to be cherished.

6. Write and Pray

We talked earlier in chapter two about letting God find us in prayer. Now, through prayer, we let Him guide us in service. This is important—especially in your own home. Remember, God is ever your guide every day and no matter how long the night, He is your guide.

> *For this God is [your] God forever and ever; He will be [your] guide*
> *even to the end (Psalm 48:14).*

When I was a child of elementary school age, I received a small gift in Sunday School. It was a small, but quite beautiful, silver cross. It was intended to be kept in a pocket or a change purse, in a place where I would see it and contact it frequently. On the back of the cross two words were engraved: "Pray always."

At the time I received this little cross, the meaning and significance of the words engraved upon it were lost upon me. But I dutifully carried that cross each day in my trouser pocket. Each day, when I reached for change, or something else in my pocket, there was the cross. And there were those words. Each night before bed, I transferred the cross to the "next day's trousers." And, in God's time, I came to learn about those words.

I learned that those two little words remind me of a very large and comforting truth: God is present, God is with me, and God hears and answers me in prayer.

Prayer is "powerful" and "effective." (See James 5:16.) God hears your prayer. (See Proverbs 15:29.) God will answer your prayer. (See Jeremiah 33:3.) Spend time in the sections titled "Implementing the Ideas in This Chapter," which follow this chapter as well as chapter four. Write and pray about the questions following both chapters. When in doubt, move toward God, move toward the light. (See John 1:5.) Be still. Listen. Trust God. And trust God's time.

Serve Through Vocation

Jesus himself "...learned about His mission while He was cutting wood and making chairs, beds and cabinets. He came as a carpenter to show us that – no matter what we do – everything can lead us to the experience of God's love. "[lxxiv]

Think back on the stories in chapter one of this book—the story of Mother Teresa and the story of Jesus' encounter with Peter and his brother. In one story: service in a far off land, in self denial and pain and suffering. In the other: disciples who drop everything in family and vocation to "follow Jesus of Nazareth." These stories are biblical lessons about the present time—the "now." The time is now to follow Him and be of service. One of the ways to find the joy of living the service driven life is to serve through your chosen vocation. How can that be, you may ask?

It is tempting in our world to separate faith, on the one hand, from work and vocation on the other; these can seem like two very different worlds. In Revelation 2:4, John writes about those who "...have abandoned the love you had at first." That love is at the core of the Christian faith. Later in the same passage, John writes about those who have made their vocation a place of idolatry—which is to say, a place where faith is lacking or absent. (See Revelation 2:14.) We are cautioned to join the two. In fact, vocation is an enormously rich mission field for our faith and service—rewarding beyond measure to those who serve.

I suggest to you six signposts on the path to serving through vocation.

1. Examine what you do and how you do it.

What goes on between your ears about your work? Do you think of yourself as worthy? Do you think of yourself as good at what you do? Do you look for the good in what you do?

Find in your profession the good in what you do and how you do it, the ways in which you help others. Find the ways in which you make others' lives better. Do you like everything about what you do daily in your vocation? Perhaps not. Despite that, serve others.

The story is told of a Deputy[lxxv] Attorney General for the State of California. This Deputy had a very important job representing "the people of the State of California." This particular Deputy sued oil companies for what were called "Reid Vapor Pressure" violations at the gasoline pump. The results of elevated pressure at the pump are devastating to air quality, but the cost of lowering "RVP" is huge and in some cases, the oil companies saw the cost of violation as worth the risk, as nothing more than a "bean counting" analysis.

Is it easy to see oneself "of service" when suing to enforce RVP standards? Perhaps. But one day, the Deputy's boss—an Assistant Attorney General— began settling or dismissing cases—strong cases—for no apparent reason. Oil companies began settling major violations with "civil penalties" that were, in truth, oil company petty cash, funds taken seemingly from the CEO's sock drawer.

The deputy turned to dark thinking. "What's the point? What I'm doing is useless and, worse, a fraud. I'm not saving the environment; I am a co-conspirator in looking the other way." Such thinking was fundamentally misguided and self-defeating. Will every avenue of service produce immediate, successful, and satisfying results? Of course not. Does that make it less "of service?" Of course not. It is one's thinking that either stymies or releases the power of service. It is within our control to find a servant mind and heart. It's within our own thinking that we can find a means to serve others in our vocation and to understand that everything—*everything*—we do can be a vessel for service. It is in this sense that *our thinking* determines the outcome.

And the deputy? He continued in his work, discouraged but determined and committed. One day, the elected attorney general—in this case, the man at the top—was changed by a vote of the people. Next day, the deputy was once again prosecuting vigorously and with enormous success and impact.

2. How are you of service through vocation?

Know that you serve through vocation. It's already happening! A lawyer helps her client through a time of great difficulty; a gardener creates beauty in the lives of those who see his or her work; a pastor offers the congregant a place of calm in the midst of a storm—a life-changing and life-saving place. What about the utility worker who brings to thousands of people the electric power necessary to their lives? Or the teacher who offers his students not just knowledge and learning, but role and success modeling. The employer who provides jobs and thereby, makes the lives of his employees and their families better. The employees who make the employer's business a success, create more jobs for more employees, and multiply productivity.

The worker in a fast food restaurant who offers the customer food, but also adds a friendly tone and a warm smile. The customer, taken aback, says this: "Thank you for making my day a little better." In that moment, in that corner of the globe, the worker is of service. It is a moment of power and of meaning. This kind of moment can happen and does happen every day, in every profession and every vocation.

3. How can you be of service through vocation?

Write and pray about the following questions: How do I now serve through vocation? Who is helped by what I do? Be kind to yourself. Do not judge and do not punish yourself. See the good in what you do. Stay open to the possibility that God wants you exactly where you are in vocation. Then move on to this: how would I like to serve through my vocation? What can I change in my attitude—and my actions—in my vocation? What can I give pro bono in what I do and to whom?

I have served on the Lawyers Committee of the Annual Conference of the United Methodist Church. Some of the most "rewarding" work I have done as a lawyer has been through this completely pro bono work—assisting over the years dozens of local churches. These churches frequently find themselves embroiled in troubling legal matters—legal matters that distract from the important and spiritual mission of these churches.

Another lawyer I know is an estate planner. He makes it a regular part of his week to visit at no charge clients and former clients who are now confined to skilled nursing homes. First on his list are seniors who have no one who can or will visit. Frequently, this lawyer shares a meal with those he visits—complete with nursing home cuisine. To a place often filled with loneliness and pain, he brings a great gift. He is changed. He is renewed.

4. Merge faith and workplace.

Ask yourself this question:

> *"Can I merge my faith—my servant's heart—with my workplace and, if necessary, preach not with words but with actions?"*

What exactly does it mean to merge your faith with your workplace? It means bringing your faith with you. It means bringing what you're learning and working on in the journey to the service driven life into the workplace.

By preaching about it and irritating your fellow workers? No. By carrying with you your faith—the meaning, power and joy you are discovering—and using that as a source of strength in your workplace, by modeling the service driven life for others to see. Imagine what would happen if you brought into your workplace the meaning you've discovered—the power and joy that is now yours. Would your fellow workers recognize you?

One of the most common ways that well-intentioned men and women of faith separate faith and vocation is by separating Sunday from the rest of the week. This separation not only removes faith from vocation, it removes faith from most of the rest of "everyday" life. How sad that is. If you leave your faith at the door as you leave your place of worship, you have left your source of strength at the door—your source of strength in vocation, your source of strength at home, your source of strength in life. God is your joy. (See Psalm 43:4.) The joy of God is your strength. (See Nehemiah 8:10.) God is a God of nearness, of presence, of inseparability. Draw near to Him and He will draw near to you. (See James 4:8.) He will draw near wherever you are, whatever challenges you face, and whenever you draw near.

5. Allow yourself to be newly empowered in vocation.

In the last section, I asked you to use your imagination. Imagine what would happen if you brought into your workplace the meaning you've discovered—the power and joy that is now yours. What would happen to your work and your work product if you thought of yourself as a man or woman of God? If you thought of yourself as worthy? If you saw yourself as fundamentally good; as loving and compassionate, filled with the capacity to forgive? If you thought of yourself as good at what you do? If you looked for the good in what you do? If you saw yourself as "of service" in vocation? As you begin to see yourself in service to clients, to customers, to students, to patients, you will bring into your life a new energy, a new peace and contentment.

Perhaps most important, as you see yourself in vocational service to your family, you will embrace a fundamental truth about what you do and how you serve. In your vocation, you support those most precious to you. That support can be an enormously loving gift. Do what you do in vocation with a servant's heart. If you allow yourself that much—that you love and serve your family in vocation—you will begin to experience a very unfamiliar peace and contentment in that part of your life. With acceptance of yourself and what you do in vocation, the floodgates will open. Not only will you experience new peace and contentment, you will find a new energy, a new passion, a new productivity in your work. This change in your own attitude and thinking is a very powerful concept. Embrace it now.

6. Write and pray.

I spoke in chapter two about seeking God and letting Him find you in prayer. Now, through prayer, let Him guide you in service through vocation. (See Psalm 48:14.) Ask God to show you how your vocation brings you closer to Him.

As you serve and love through home and family, and through vocation, you will begin to find a contentment, a peace, and a joy unknown which will free you truly to love your "neighbor." The floodgates have opened. You have sought God and He has found you. You have looked at yourself and changed your thinking about yourself and your priorities. You have heard the loving commandment to love others as God loves you and the invitation to "complete joy." The question now is not "how can I serve?" Rather, the question now is "how do I feel led to serve?" Service is not between you and me, or even between you and a friend or pastor. It is between you and God. The exciting thing is that having drawn close to God and re-ordered your thinking and your priorities, God opens many doors and shows us many avenues of service: a church choir, a praise team, lay leader, creative writing shared with others, reading to a shut-in, sharing with a friend about things that matter, or in simply, without condition, loving another. For it is in love and forgiveness that we truly serve God.

Serve Through Loving Your "Neighbor"

Here am I; send me (Isaiah 6:8)!
Go and do likewise (Luke 10:29-37).

What you will find as you embrace the service driven life is that you have moved into life with new energy and passion and joy. Service is no longer a question. It is who you are—a man or woman of love and compassion and forgiveness, with an irrepressible call to serve others and driven by God's two "greatest" commandments: "Love God with all your heart, soul, mind and strength; and love and serve your neighbor as God has loved you." (See Mark 12:28-31 and Luke 10:25-28.)

91

And who is your "neighbor?" That question is answered in the parable of the Good Samaritan:

> But wanting to justify himself, the lawyer asked Jesus: "And who is my neighbor?" Jesus replied: "A man was going down from Jerusalem to Jericho, and fell into the hands of robbers, who stripped him, beat him, and went away, leaving him half dead. Now by chance a priest was going down that road; and when he saw him, he passed by on the other side. So likewise a Levite, when he came to the place and saw him, passed by on the other side. But a Samaritan while traveling came near him; and when he saw him, he was moved. He went to him and bandaged his wounds, having poured oil and wine on them. Then he put him on his own animal, brought him into an inn and took care of him. The next day he took out two denarii, gave them to the innkeeper and said, 'Take care of him; and when I come back, I will repay you whatever more you spend.' Which of these three, do you think, was a neighbor to the man who fell into the hands of the robbers?" He said, "The one who showed him mercy." Jesus said to him, "Go and do likewise" (Luke 10:29-37).

The key to this parable is the lawyer's answer, "The one who showed him mercy." The parable is about what the Samaritan *did*—as neighbor—for his neighbor.

In this chapter, we move out of ourselves and toward our neighbor. We seek opportunities to serve, opportunities to go and do likewise. The opportunities are limitless.

Here are some suggestions to help you embrace your service to neighbor.

1. Make that contact.

Make that call to a mentoring program for kids at risk, to the food bank with empty shelves, to the home for seniors looking for readers and performing artists. (Please see Appendix 2 for a list of specific areas of service.) Make that call or send that e-mail to the service organization you've thought about for years but have never seriously pursued. Perhaps you are drawn to the service club whose members build clean water pumps and tanks in India and other countries around the globe, or the service organization working toward the eradication of the wild polio virus active now in just three countries on the face of the planet.

Ask the question now: "How do I serve?" Answer it honestly. Then take a first step. Watch out for that thinking that separates us from meaning and joy. "I don't have time." "If only…" "Nothing I do is worthy." That thinking is, and those responses are, *off* the table for good! If need be, re-read and re-work chapter three, changing your thinking and priorities, and work on implementing its ideas. And then be open to the amazing places—literally and figuratively—to which you will be led!

2. Tap your creative side and see what God moves in you.

Perhaps you need to renew the creative side of you or touch the eternal in you—with music, poetry, great literature. Perhaps your service includes bringing great joy, peace, and beauty to others through your creativity, a time when you touch the eternal in all of us, a time when God speaks to you and to those you serve. Play the piano at a retirement home filled with seniors who would love to hear you play. Read to that senior who can no longer read on her own, the senior who thinks all have forgotten her. Sing to God in a praise team in a local church that has attracted you. Come into His presence with a joyful song. (See Psalms 100:2.) Sing the music of "…those who are climbing to the light."[lxxvi] God loves a joyful song. The prophet Zephaniah said, "God rejoices over you in song. The Lord God Himself is exulting over you…in song!" (See Zephaniah 3:17.)

Be open to serving in ways that may never have occurred to you before. I know a very good and successful lawyer[lxxvii] in another state. He is also a juggler. He rides a unicycle and juggles at the same time. He has an "act" which is very un-lawyer-like and very funny. It would be "stand up" comedy if the juggler wasn't sitting down on a unicycle during act. The "act" is performed mostly for family. One day, this lawyer-juggler was invited to bring his act to a local retirement home. The lawyer juggler wasn't sure about it; why would anybody there want to see him do his act? But he did it; he unicycled and juggled for a hundred seniors, complete with a quite wonderful stream of commentary and jokes. The lawyer-juggler had a ball and so did the crowd! The crowd smiled and roared and cheered. And cheered some more. For those moments in time, the lawyer-juggler brought great joy to a place not always joyful. To a place filled with stories of loneliness and pain, he brought a great gift of love and service to neighbor. He was changed, he was renewed.

Look inside for what is within you, for the gifts that God has given you—gifts with which you are uniquely equipped to love and serve. Those gifts are there in each of us. Trust in them. Know the power, the simplicity, and the joy of service. Trust God.

3. Spend some time with the stories of service following the chapters of this book.

In the stories of service in this book, you will find inspiration and meaning, power and joy. Read slowly, thinking and feeling about the people in the stories, those served and those who serve. Be open to the stories that speak to you. Pick a story and write down how you feel about the story. What draws you to the story? Do you see God moving in the story? Is there joy in the story, for those served and those who serve?

If you haven't done so already, go to Appendix 2 and peruse the avenues of service. Think about the many programs and projects described there. You may be amazed at the power and joy you find traveling along these "avenues." From food banks to mentoring, from surfers healing to therapeutic riding, from low-cost housing to the adoption of kids no one wanted into loving homes. These are stories of servants serving neighbors, not as conqueror or boss, nor as victim or trampled rug. Rather, these are stories of humble servants bringing to those they serve love and compassion—and great joy—and servants finding for themselves a joy without measure.

Be still, listen. Be open to God moving in you. He *will* lead you in His time.

4. Write and pray.

I spoke in chapter two about seeking God and letting Him find you in prayer. Now, through prayer, let Him guide you in service to your neighbor. (See Psalm 48:14.) Prayer is "powerful" and "effective." (See James 5:16.)

> *God hears your prayer. (Proverbs 15:29.)*
>
> *God will answer your prayer. (Jeremiah 33:3.)*

Be still. Listen. Trust God. And trust God's time.

Still not sure where you are led in service? This journey is about seeking His will in your life. Focus below on nine ways to know where God is leading you in service through home and family, through vocation, and through neighbor.

Nine Ways to Know Where God Is Leading You to Serve

1. Spend time in prayer.

God is ever your guide. Let Him guide you in service. Remember that wonderful hymn—"Guide me, O Thou Great Jehovah…" There is a reason this is one of the most popular hymns on the planet. "Guide me, lead me all my journey through… thou my strength and shield."

Pray about your service and where God might be leading you. Remember the biblical and scriptural foundation of service. During the last supper, Jesus washed the disciples' feet as a servant to a master. (See John 13:2-9.) And after supper, Jesus gave to the disciples a new commandment, "That you love one another as I have loved you. Just as I have loved you, you also should love one another. (See John 13:34-35 and John 15:12.) I am giving you this commandment so that you may love one another" (John 15:17).

Like Jesus, in the morning, while it is still dark, get up and go out to a deserted place. Pray. (See Mark 1:35.) You need not have the most articulate and comprehensive prayer ever written, simply open yourself up to God's presence and guidance. Prayer is simply the "linking up of the soul and mind and heart to God."[lxxviii]

Years ago my father—a Methodist preacher and author—told me a story about prayer. I've never forgotten it. "While walking through the woods one day, I was surprised to hear a child's voice. I followed the sound, trying in vain to understand the child's words. When I spotted a boy perched on a rock, I realized why his words had made no sense: The child was repeating the alphabet. 'Why are you saying your ABC's so many times?' I asked him.

The child replied, 'I'm saying my prayers.'

I couldn't help but laugh. 'Prayers? All I hear is the alphabet.'

Patiently the child explained, 'Well, I don't know all the words, so I give God the letters. God knows what I'm trying to say.'"

This story reminds us that our prayers are, in a sense, for us, not for God. God knows what you are going through. The content of your prayer comes from your heart, not from your words. God knows what you are trying to say! How comforting that is! God knows what you need before you ask Him! (See Matthew 6:8.) With prayer, you say that you are willing to be helped, willing to listen, and willing to hear God's guidance and His will. He may come to you in the still small voice, the sheer sound of silence, or the "knowing" that appears without warning and in God's own time. In prayer, He will come to you. Know it, be in it, feel it. And remember that "no one who has ever experienced God in prayer has *ever found anything more joyful,* not even owning half the world."[lxxix]

2. Spend time in scripture.

At the end of chapters two through five, you will find sections called "Focus on Scripture." As you feel the need or the call, return to these sections. Spend time reading the full context of the cited scripture. Be aware when you feel called to read certain passages or when you find yourself, almost by accident, in a particularly helpful passage. It's probably not an accident. You may want to highlight a passage that you read a thousand times before, but this time the passage speaks to you clearly and in a new and comforting way—as if a ray of light is breaking through the clouds. Allow yourself to be led in your time, and His time, with scripture. Let your reading take you to unexpected places! Let God take you to unexpected places!

Perhaps now spend some time in the "book of songs." The book of Psalms, also called the Psalter, is a truly glorious collection of song, prayer, liturgy, and poetry, passionate and heartfelt. The Psalter is divided into five small books. Nearly half the 150 psalms are attributed to King David. The psalms were originally intended to be sung. David's songs are truly from the heart, filled with the range of human emotion—from despair to joy, from doubt to faith, fear to the confidence of God's presence and protection. Scholars have categorized each of the psalms as:

- a praise psalm
- a lament
- a song of ascent
- a wisdom or teaching psalm

Martin Luther wrote that the book of Psalms "might well be called a little Bible. In it is comprehended most beautifully and briefly everything that is in the entire Bible. It is really a fine enchiridion or hand-book. In fact, I have a notion that the Holy Spirit wanted to take the trouble himself to compile a short Bible and book of examples for all Christendom and for all saints, so that anyone who could not read the whole Bible would here have anyway almost an entire summary of it, comprised in one little book."[lxxx]

As you consider God's call on you in service, I call your attention to four of my favorite psalms: Psalm 121, Psalm 145, Psalm 46, and Psalm 16. These are songs of trust and joy and confidence, "mountaintop" moments. These four psalms can teach much about the journey you are on.

One of the most powerful songs of "ascent" is Psalm 121. The "ascent" psalms are thought to have been sung in ancient times while approaching the temple in Jerusalem. Psalm 121 is also referred to as a "trust" psalm: trust in His presence, trust that He watches over you, and trust in His help for you.

Verse two speaks eloquently of the place from whence your help "cometh" and verses three through eight reassure no less than six times that He will keep you and He will watch over you.

> *I will lift up mine eyes unto the hills, from whence cometh my help.*
>
> *My help cometh from the LORD, which made heaven and earth.*
>
> *He will not suffer thy foot to be moved: He that keepeth thee will not*
>
> *slumber. Behold, He that keepeth Israel shall neither slumber nor sleep.*
>
> *The LORD is thy keeper: the LORD is thy shade upon thy right hand.*
>
> *The sun shall not smite thee by day, nor the moon by night.*
>
> *The LORD shall preserve thee from all evil: He shall preserve thy soul.*
>
> *The LORD shall preserve thy going out and thy coming in from this*
>
> *time forth, and even for evermore (Psalm 121 KJV).*

As you seek His will, not yours, as you seek your path of service—serving God by serving others—rest in the assurance that God is with you, and will help you, and He watches over you on your journey.

Psalm 145 is a psalm of praise. In it we are reminded that "God is near to all who call on Him, to all who call on Him in truth" (verse 18). In seeking the service driven life, you are coming to God in truth, honesty, and humility. Rest in the assurance that He is near you on your path. Feel how that feels. You are not alone on your path!

Psalm 145 can also remind you of God's unconditional love and compassion:

> *The Lord is gracious and merciful, slow to anger and abounding in*
>
> *steadfast love. The Lord is good to all, and His compassion is over all*
>
> *that He has made (Psalm 145:8-9).*

As you seek your path of service, take refuge in the love and compassion that God has for you and your determination to live in a place of love and compassion for yourself and others. His "abounding" love is ever-present for you—now as you seek a new path—and evermore. Ever present as you are commanded to "go and love others as I have loved you." You are invited, commanded out of God's love and compassion, to go to a place of great joy, a place where His joy is in you and your joy is "complete." (See John 15:9-11.)

Among the "wisdom and teaching" psalms is Psalm 46. In it we hear the reassuring words of the psalmist: God is your "refuge and strength" and a "very present help" (Psalm 46:1-2). Therefore, fear not. The river in this passage is the poet's image of God's presence:

> *God is our refuge and strength, a very present help in trouble.*
>
> *Therefore will not we fear, though the earth be removed, and though the mountains be carried into the midst of the sea;*
>
> *Though the waters thereof roar and be troubled, though the mountains shake with the swelling thereof.*
>
> *There is a river, the streams whereof shall make glad the city of God, the holy place of the tabernacles of the most High.*
>
> *God is in the midst of the city; it shall not be moved: God will help it when the morning dawns. (Psalm 46:1-5).*

Not only is God with you now, He is a "very present help" (Psalm 46:1, 7, 11). "Be still, and know that He is God" (Psalm 46:10). And listen!

Finally, turn to Psalm 16, often referred to as a Miktam of David, a song of trust and security in God. This is a particularly intriguing psalm, partly because David's words are quoted in the New Testament in Acts 2:28. Simply pause on your journey to feel the power and strength of David's words:

> *You show me the path of life; in your presence there is fullness of joy. (Psalm 16:11; Acts 2:28).*

He is present on your path; He will make known your path! He will fill you with joy! Know this "confidently" (Acts 2:29) and "with certainty" (Acts 2:36).

3. Let's return for a moment to Revelation 3: Hear God's voice.

> *Behold, I stand at the door and knock. If any hear my voice and open*

the door, I will come in to him and sup with him and he with me. (Revelation 3:20 KJV).

"If you hear my voice" doesn't mean God *may* speak to you. It means God *is* speaking to you. The question is whether or not *you hear* Him! His invitation to come in to you and "sup" or fellowship with you and you with Him is an invitation to an intimate relationship with Him. Listen for that voice, whatever form it may take; listen for that quiet knowing; be still, and know that He is God. (Psalm 46:10.) He is present (Psalm 46:11) and is your help and your refuge (Psalm 46:1; Psalm 121:1-2, 8).

4. Find a community of faith.

There are many churches and communities of faith that can be of help and support in your journey—as you spend time in prayer and in scripture, and as you seek to hear God's voice in your life. Try several churches. Be open. If you've been uncomfortable in a church in the past, it's even more important to try several churches, perhaps more than several churches. Look at the mission statements of the churches you visit. Look for something like this: "We are a community of faith seeking intentionally to live out God's unconditional love for all persons...our purpose is to grow in our Christian faith through prayer and study, worship and fellowship, as we witness to God's healing power in our community and the world by serving our neighbor." Look through the church websites of the many churches included in the "Avenues of Service" in Appendix 2. If you're comfortable, pay a visit.

Listen as you visit. Listen to your own heart and pay attention to how it feels to be in such a place. Listen for God's voice, listen for His lead. Many have been "strangely warmed"—as was John Wesley—in the midst of a community of faith. Be open to that. Draw near to God and He will draw near to you. And He will lead you.

As you search for a community of faith, a church home, beware. There are many Christian churches out there where service is preached. There are also many Christian churches out there where fear, doubt, and confusion are preached.

As a Methodist "preacher's kid," I grew up seeing much of the soft underbelly of the organized church. Not just the petty, oh-so-human bickering, but the need to win souls to make or increase a budget; the need to cement membership. In some ways, I felt as the exile to Babylon, asked to "sing the Lord's song in a foreign land" (Psalm 137:4). In today's world, the twisting and manipulation of scripture for personal gain—designating one's reading of scripture as the *only* reading—is rampant. If you send money, He will richly reward you, or so it goes—financially and with meaning in your life. And, conveniently enough, here's the address to send your "love gift," your investment in your very own future. Boy, are you going to feel a whole lot better having unloaded your life savings to this ministry. Beware of such fraud, and it is that. It is the most blatant form of "religion that hurts."[lxxxi]

Sometimes, Christian churches preach fear or try to scare people into faith by offering biblical readings not subject to thought or prayer. In the section on "What Service Is Not" in chapter two, we saw that God is not hovering over humankind, eager to pour out His wrath on those who live for themselves. Romans 3:24 says that believers are justified freely by His **grace** through the redemption that came by Christ Jesus. Salvation is either through the gift of His grace or it is not. God's grace alone brings us into a relationship with God. God has acted in Jesus Christ and we need only respond in faith—not as a condition of the gift, but as a sign of the gift already given! [lxxxii]

Then there is the dogma that applies a litmus test to the gospel of John 3:7, that we need to be saved in a certain way, implying that if we are not "*born again*" in the approved manner and fashion, salvation cannot be ours. In the tradition of Paul and of Luther and of John Wesley, salvation is a "turning around, leaving one orientation for another. It may be sudden and dramatic, or gradual and cumulative." In any event, it is for us a joyful rebirth, a new life in Christ, indeed a regeneration.[lxxxiii] And in that rebirth we experience God's "justifying grace"—His forgiveness, a new peace and joy and love.

Yes, this time of justification, of salvation, is also a time of repentance— "turning away" from behaviors rooted in sin and toward a life that expresses God's love. It is this expression of God's love that draws us into a service driven life where we live loving others as God has loved us. Yes, this is "repentance"—but it is repentance based neither in dogma nor in fear. It is based in love.

If the time feels appropriate and right, perhaps go now to God in prayer. Find a quiet place—whether it's "in the morning, while it is still very dark;" whether in a "deserted place;" (Mark 1:35) or at "the gloaming" in a favorite place of nature—go to God now with this prayer. If it helps you, say the prayer out loud, allowing the words to flow out of your heart and center to a present God, a God of goodness, of hope, and of joy. He is present, my friend, and He hears you.

> *Dear God, you stand at the door and knock. I hear your voice. And I open the door. I invite you into my heart now...that I might find a new life in Christ. Help me to feel your gift of grace to me in my life... and the power of your love, your forgiveness and your compassion... your nearness and your presence... your inseparability from me, in my life. Teach me to live a life that expresses your love, forgiveness, and compassion, that I may be a man or woman of God, loving you with all my heart and soul, mind and strength, and loving others as you have loved me. Teach me to experience in its fullness the complete joy, the boundless joy, of serving you by serving others. In thy steadfast love and grace, Amen and Amen.*

If you have just prayed this prayer, it is even more important that you seek a community of faith to love and support you in your new journey. As you do so, remember this above all: love and fear are inconsistent. Fear is never enough to give us peace, although it may get us out of bed each day for some period of time. It is in no way a satisfactory answer or a lasting solution to any question.

I do not believe that God, a loving God, offers us fear. God offers us love and forgiveness. That is why we are enjoined not to fear Him, but to trust Him wholly, fear nothing, hope ever, and look ever up to Him.

We are commanded to love God and to love and serve others. And what does God offer us, indeed, promise us? He promises to love us and to care for us and to be with us forever. If you turn to Genesis 9:8-17, you will see that in this text the word *covenant*, or *promise*, is mentioned eight times in most translations.

It is important to seek out a community of faith that can be of help and support, love and care, in your journey and on your path. Following your path to meaning, power and joy can be much enriched by a community of men and women that loves and supports its congregants, its neighbors, and you.

One of the wonderful things about finding a loving and supportive community of faith is that you will find a virtual explosion of opportunities to serve. As your faith and your relationship with God grow, perhaps you'll want to serve in a music and praise program, an outreach, evangelism program, habitat for humanity, lay visitation of those in need or who are hurting. Or perhaps yours will be a call to teach kids and youth in Sunday School or kids/youth groups mid-week. What a joyful place to spend time in spiritual growth, with youngsters eager to learn about God!

One of the wonderful things about teaching in such settings is that it forces you to examine your faith and spend time in scripture. It forces you to articulate your faith and your love of God. And in the end, the people you serve, young and old alike, will see in you a true man or woman of God, one who is being transformed in love and service. The impact on those you teach will be surprising, unexpected, and, dare I say it, miraculous!

Look through the church websites of the many churches included in the "Avenues of Service" attached as Appendix. 2 There are among these churches many loving and supportive communities of faith.

5. Re-read the Stories of Service.

I hope you've been inspired by the Stories of Service following chapters two through four. There is power in "story," in the picture we see of others who serve God, their families, and the people around them. At the end of selfless service, there are changed lives. You may want to look more closely at one particular story that caught your interest and spoke to you. Here's a quick review of those stories to refresh your memory here:

- The story of the surgeon, as he sees the face of God
- The adoptive parents, strengthened in faith
- Janet and the food drive and the power of her changed thinking
- The story of Henry and the power of changed priorities
- The stories of mentoring and the great joy in those served and in those serving. "Can there be any doubt that through my service, I am changed?" said the mentor.

Perhaps one of the stories in the text of the chapters in this book caught your attention, moved you deeply. Perhaps the story of polio eradication, of clean water, the story of the Deputy AG and service through vocation, the visitations of the estate planner, the lawyer juggler, vegetables on a picnic table. Perhaps the joyful story of Peter...

Trust God. He will lead you in service...

6. *Use the scripture and questions for writing and prayer following chapters four and five.*

There is a wealth of treasure to be found in the scriptures that follow each chapter, especially those in chapter four. Here you will find specific questions designed to help you find the joy in the service driven life. After chapter five, you will find scriptural focus and questions designed to help you find your own path of service.

7. *Spend some time reading "The Avenues of Service" in the appendix.*

"The Avenues of Service" coincide with this chapter and are intended as a resource and reference. The service opportunities available to you are unlimited, especially as you are open to hearing God's voice and open to presenting Him with your willingness to serve. I want to encourage you to travel down these avenues, spend some time considering how others serve their "neighbors"—changing the lives of those they touch and their own lives! This list is not exhaustive, of course, but it a good place to begin. You may serve at food banks, mentoring and tutoring programs, the myriad programs and projects of large churches, small churches, denominational churches, independent churches, service organizations like Rotary, Kiwanis, Lions, Exchange Club, therapeutic riding center, surfers healing for autistic children, adoptive services, assistance for children victimized by war, conflict and natural disaster, services for victims of domestic violence and abuse, low-income and means-based housing, prison ministries, Catholic charities, Boy and Girl Scouts, Salvation Army, Good Will Industries, volunteers to homes for the deaf in Mexico, volunteers to serve the "invisible children" victimized by war in Uganda, alternative schools for young people struggling with abuse, addiction and other crises.

Be still. Listen. Be open to God moving in you. He will lead you in His time. Trust Him.

8. *Write about your path of service.*

Then write about your path of service—service through home and family, service through vocation, and service through neighbor. Start with a writing tablet or a spiral notebook or simply 3 blank sheets of paper. This is your path of service journal. At the top of the first page write: "Serving through Home & Family." At the top of the second page write: "Serving through Vocation." Finally, on the third page: "Serving through Neighbor."

Over the next several days, or even weeks, keep your journal with you; write as you feel called to write. Don't worry about style, grammar, syntax, or how much you are writing. Just write as moved. Add what you find yourself thinking about—ways in which you now serve or things you'd like to do differently. How would you like to serve? How do you feel moved to serve? Sit with it. Enjoy the process. Take your time.

If you need help with your writing, return to the scripture and the questions for writing and prayer following chapters four and five. Find a place of quiet contemplation. Pray and then write. Feel the comfort of God moving in you, in His time—the only time and timing that is unerring and filled with His blessings.

Be kind to yourself. It has been said, "The highest form of wisdom is kindness."[lxxxiv] That includes kindness to you! In chapter three, I talked about loving and forgiving yourself as God loves and forgives you. Each of us must give ourselves the gift of love and compassion. Now is the time to feel that gift—to feel love and compassion for yourself. Not tomorrow, *now*.

Feel what it says about you that you are truly willing to examine yourself honestly—that you truly seek a close and intimate relationship with God, that you seek to love and forgive as God loves and forgives you. Feel what it says about you that you seek to serve God by serving through family, vocation, and neighbor. Others will know you (and you will know yourself) by what you believe about God and about yourself. They will know who you are by what you do. (See Matthew 7:16.) This is an exciting time for you!

9. However small it may seem, take action today.

Remember that no gift is poor if it expresses the true love of the giver.[lxxxv] Start down a different road, a different avenue, than the one you've been traveling. Go outside of yourself now. Move toward the light. And remember those words from the first chapter of the gospel of John: "The light shines in the darkness and the darkness cannot overcome it" (John 1:5).

The moment you spend today may be life-changing for you and for another human soul. Smile at the homeless person outside the convenience store. You know the one—the one with whom you've avoided eye contact for weeks or months. Give him your pocket change. Or engage him. Direct him to a local church or pastor who will connect him with a local food bank or family assistance ministry. Or better yet, connect him yourself with such a place of love and compassion. Feel the power and the meaning of who you are and what you are doing with yourself and with others.

A young woman approached me after a lecture I once gave the week before Christmas in a large hotel. While attending the lecture, the woman had been feeling depressed and lonely about the Christmas season. During the lecture, she said she had felt a sudden shift in herself about Christmas and the season and she "knew"—"almost as if somebody had put the thought in [her] mind"—what she needed to do. At that moment, the woman had decided she would not add to the 450 billion dollars spent each year by Americans during the Christmas season. (Orange County Register, Dec. 30, 2006, Part 2, Page 2[i]). Rather, this woman took the small sum she had set aside for Christmas spending and gave it—wholly, deliberately, and with a true servant's heart—to an organization seeking funds to provide clean water to kids who have none.

This young woman's decision seemed to her at the time a small gesture, a small act. But the impact of her decision on *her* was both immediate and profound. The woman was led to become a volunteer in the organization to which she had contributed her Christmas funds and she is now a key player in the fight to bring clean water to every child on the face of the planet. She has never forgotten the "knowing"—the presence of God—she felt on that day, at Christmas time.

What does this story tell us? Two things. First, when you feel moved to act in service, act. Even if it seems a small act or gesture. The young woman in this story took action; she began with a financial donation. There is service in that. But that was only the beginning. As her path of service became clear, Jesus' admonition to "go and do as I have done" was no longer an idle phrase. This woman of service came to know that it was the gift of herself that truly changes lives—the lives of those she serves and her own life. Only God knows the full length and breadth of the amazing path you are starting down with that first step of service.

Second, be open to God moving in your life. When He does move—and He *will* move—embrace it. Go and do as He has done. Come alive in it. Advance confidently, knowing that when you serve, you will "abide in His love, His joy will be in you and your joy will be complete." (See John 15:9-11.)

Avenues of Service[lxxxvii]

I've inserted an appendix at the back of the book which lists the names of nonprofit organizations that need volunteers. Each place of service includes contact information, a brief explanation of the service, and a website.

Please take time to peruse prayerfully the appendix. You will find a list of places to serve.

> *Be still. Listen. Be open to God moving in you. He will lead you in His time. He will make known to you your path; He will fill you with joy in His presence. (See Psalm 16:11 and Acts 2:28.)* Trust Him.

Implementing the Ideas in This chapter

Focus on Scripture

You will know them by their fruits. (Matthew 7:16). You will know who they are by what they do.

You show me the path; in your presence there is fullness of joy. (Psalm 16:11; Acts 2:28).

Here am I; send me (Isaiah 6:8)

Go and do likewise. (Luke 10:37)

I've included additional scripture for your personal research and study in Appendix 1, at the end of this book.

Chapter Review

Focus on these specific ways—covered in this chapter—to know where God is leading and to discover your path of service. If you think it would be helpful, return to each of these topics in the chapter.

Serve through home and family:

- Words can love/words can hurt

- Remember Henry

- Be a force for love and forgiveness in your home

- Preach the gospel and when necessary use words

- Think differently; do differently

- Write and pray

Serve through vocation:

- Examine what you do and how you do it

- How you are of service through vocation?

- How can you be of service through vocation?

- Merge faith and workplace

- Allow yourself to be newly empowered in vocation

- Write and pray

Serve through neighbor:

- Make that contact

- Tap your creative side and see what God moves in you.

- Spend some time with the stories of service following the chapters of this book; spend some time with the avenues of service in chapter five

- Write and pray

Nine ways to know where God is leading you in service:

- Spend time in prayer

- Spend time in scripture

- Hear God's voice

- Find a community of faith

- Re-read the stories of service
- Use the scripture and questions for writing and prayer following this chapter and chapter four
- Spend some time on the avenues of service
- Write about your path of service
- Take action today!

Questions to Write and Pray About

How do I serve through home and family? How would I like to serve through home and family?

_____

_____

_____

How much time do I spend in prayer about my family and my home? Would it be comforting to spend more of such time? Can I be open to God's guidance?

_____

_____

_____

Can I be a force for love and forgiveness in my home? In my words? In what I do?

_____

_____

_____

How can I relate to Henry's story?

_____

_____

_____

What have I missed in my life and the lives of those I love as a result of my thinking and my priorities?

_____

_____

_____

How would it feel to me to model in my home the two greatest commandments?

_____

_____

_____

How do I serve through my vocation?

_____

_____

_____

How would I like to serve through my vocation?

_____

_____

_____

What do I do at work, and how do I do it?

_____

_____

_____

What can I change in my attitude and approach to my vocation?

_____

_____

_____

What would it mean for me, a man or woman of faith, if I merged faith and vocation?

_____

_____

_____

What steps can I take so as not to separate faith and vocation?

_____

_____

_____

How do I serve my "neighbors," those I know and those I have never met?

_____

_____

_____

How would I like to serve my "neighbors?"

_____

_____

_____

What specific service contacts have I wanted to make but put off?

_____

_____

_____

What is my creative side? What am I good at but have not pursued?

_____

_____

_____

How can I serve others by sharing the gifts God has given me?

_____

_____

_____

When God stands at the door and knocks, do I open the door and sup with Him? Do I allow Him to lead me to service…in joy, energy, love, and passion?

_____

_____

_____

Can I be patient with myself as I strive to embrace the service driven life, its power, meaning, and joy?

_____

_____

_____

Which of the stories of service in this book moved me?

_____

_____

_____

What was I feeling when I read the story?

_____

_____

_____

If I could pick any service project I've heard about in this book, or elsewhere, which would it be?

_____

_____

_____

Have I ever felt God's still small voice?

_____

_____

_____

Have I ever felt a quiet "knowing" about something?

_____

_____

_____

Am I open to God moving in my life and leading me in service?

_____

_____

_____

What service organizations have I heard about and wanted to know more about?

_____

_____

_____

What action can I take now to learn more about the service opportunities to which I am drawn?

_____

_____

_____

What is the path of service uniquely mine?

_____

_____

_____

Chapter 6

Living the Service Driven Life
with Meaning, Power and Joy

Be patient and gentle with yourself. In the pages of this book, you have been asked to look at and to take action on some difficult things. You've been asked to look at your spiritual center and to ask some very hard questions about that. You've been asked to seek God and let Him find you, which for many flies in the face of years of resistance and doubt. You've been asked to challenge some fundamental assumptions about yourself and to change your thinking and your priorities. You've been asked to seek ways to serve others in every part of your life—through family and home, through vocation, and through neighbor. You've been asked to discover your true path of service so that your joy may be "complete."

All of this takes time. Perhaps having reached this point in this book, you'll want to return to the four sections on "Implementing the Ideas in This Chapter." As you work to implement the ideas in this book, be patient and gentle with yourself. Practice love and compassion for yourself. Revel in the comfort of God's presence, His guidance, His love and forgiveness, the knowledge that you are not alone in the journey. You are not alone, period.

I will lift up my eyes to the hills from whence cometh my help. My help comes from [God] who made heaven and earth (Psalm 121:1-2 KJV).

The Lord is my keeper; your shade at your right hand. The sun shall not smite you by day, nor the moon by night (Psalm 121:5-6 KJV).

The Lord will keep your going out and your coming in from this time forth...and for evermore (Psalm 121:8 KJV).

Again, be patient with yourself. Enjoy the journey. Meaning, empowerment, and great joy await—joy unimaginable in common days.

It's About *Your* Life

Service has been a part of my life for a very long time. Many years ago, I found myself "of service" quite by accident, or so I thought. I saw many people helped and lives changed through a service organization, a mentoring and tutoring program, and through service of various shapes and descriptions. I saw God moving in the lives of those served. I saw joy beyond measure in the magic and miracle of service. I saw people's lives changed, often transformed.

And yet something was not right. Something was missing. In some ways, I was in service, yet I could not seem to find the meaning, the power, the joy in my own life. I had many blessings in my life, but I felt empty, without purpose, without power, and certainly without joy. Because I had many blessings in my life, I felt guilt about feeling empty and ashamed to talk about it. In my emptiness, I lived for years upon years in a dark and lonely place. Finally, humbled and discouraged, I took the suggestion of a pastor I trusted. I prayed a simple prayer. I asked God for help. "Please, help me, God." That was my prayer. I prayed it again. For a very long time, I prayed it. On my knees, I prayed it. I prayed it when I woke up and I prayed it when I went to bed.

In His time, not mine, help came. It's been said that the night is darkest just before the dawn. One early morning, in the darkest part of night, I heard His voice unmistakably in two powerful passages of scripture to which I was drawn. I've talked about these passages in the pages of this book:

> *Behold, I stand at the door and knock. Open the door and I will come in to you and sup with you and you with me (Revelation 3:20 KJV).*

> *This is my commandment, that you love one another as I have loved you (John 15:12). If you keep My commandment, you will abide in my love. I have said these things to you so that My joy may be in you and that your joy may be complete. (John 15:10-11).*

I shared with you in chapters two and five about being open and listening for God's voice. On that dark September night, in the thickest part of night, I heard God's voice and I knew it. I began to move toward the light. I was led to a journey, not a destination. And that journey was about moving, changing, and then finding meaning, purpose, and great joy!

In time, I have come to know this: you will fully understand and embrace the service driven life only when you understand that it is about you and about meaning, power and joy in *your* life. It is about *your* relationship with God, about God moving in *your* life. The service driven life is about you, with God's help, changing *your* thinking and *your* priorities. It is about finding "complete" joy in *your* life.

Your service is not only about the blessings you bestow on others. It is about finding an abundant life—a life worth living. In service, there are moments of frustration and pain and heartache. Then there are those moments of triumph. Those who have lived it know that there is nothing quite like mentoring and tutoring a student at-risk who graduates with honors; nothing quite like those moments spent with a child in an orphanage in South Mexico, a child who had never received a Christmas present—*till there was you.* Nothing quite like an unexpected moment of love and compassion and renewal with those most precious—your spouse, your child, your family. Love and forgiveness communicated in a quiet moment—in a touch, a simple smile and look, a kind and loving word. These are the moments when you will know *exactly* why you do what you do. And that what you do is life-changing; changing the lives of those you serve—*and changing your own life.*

When you understand the meaning and power in who you are and what you do, the question of service is no longer a question. It is an answer filled with meaning, purpose, energy, and great joy. We serve because we are commanded to do so in a loving and God-given commandment. We serve, abiding in His love—that "His joy may be in us" and "[our] joy may be complete." (See John 15:9-11.) There is indeed great joy in service.[lxxxviii] And we find ourselves with a passionate and powerful commitment to all that is good in ourselves and in others. The powerful play goes on and *you* may contribute a verse![lxxxix] How exciting that is!

The Journey of the Service Driven Life

In chapter three, we talked about a life filled with love and compassion, a life in which love presides over fear. Does that mean that by embracing the service driven life you will never experience fear? No. What it does mean is that when "the faintest tremor of fear"[xc] appears, you can find your way back to strength and joy. How? By simply drawing near to God. By taking a few moments to revisit your thinking and priorities, resting in the knowledge that your joy is in God and in service, and knowing that your joy is complete in God and service.

The service driven life is not a problem-free, easy life. It is by definition focused outside of ourselves and our egos. For many, it is counterintuitive to what we've been taught and, therefore, when we find ourselves stuck in old thinking—when doubt and fear intrude—we may experience many of the feelings we thought we had left behind. But when we work to embrace the service driven life, we find rewards beyond anything we could have imagined.

We've talked a lot about our "thinking" in this book. In seeking to live with purpose and meaning, we are often in our thinking our own worst enemies. Does it seem too late? Too much work? Too much change? If you cannot change your thinking yet, come out of your head to the center of your being and see how it feels. Draw near to God and watch and feel Him draw near to you.

It has been said that "before sunlight can shine through a window, the blinds must be raised." [xci] Raising the blinds requires a deliberate act or acts. Do one thing today, anonymously, that will make someone else's life better. Plant a shade tree under which you will never sit. Today, "follow Him." And know this:

> *"Your power to help others lives will soon bring*
> *its delight, even when, at first, the help to yourselves*
> *may seem too late to bring you joy."* [xcii]

Most of all, my friend, do not underestimate the power of a truly service driven life. If it seems counterintuitive, simply "go with it" till it feels intuitive, until you truly believe that only those among us who seek and discover how to serve will ever be truly happy. Embrace the power of a truly service driven life and watch what happens—in every part of your life!

In the service driven life, we find ourselves living with meaning, with power and passion, with great joy, and with God. *That* is what it means to embrace the service driven life. And *that* is what it means to be fully alive.

> *"Yesterday has gone. Tomorrow has not yet come ...*
> *We have only today."*
> –Mother Teresa[xciii]

Let us begin!

APPENDIX 1

FOCUS ON SCRIPTURE

Chapter 1 The Service Driven Life

Matthew 1:18-22; Mark 1:16-20.

Chapter 2 Discover the Meaning of the Service Driven Life

Genesis 1:1; Revelation 3:20; James 4:8; James 1:6-7; Hebrews 11:1-3; Psalm 42:1; Psalm 145:18; Luke 15:3-6; Isaiah 41:9-10; Psalm 121; Mark 1:14-39, 16-21; Mark 1:35; Mark 1:36-39; James 5:13; John 14:1-2; Mark 1:36-39; Psalm 46:10; James 4:8; Psalm 145:18; Luke 15:3-6; Zephaniah 3:17; Isaiah 55:6; Isaiah 55:1-3; 1 Kings 8:56-58; Isaiah 43:1; Isaiah 41:9-10; John 21:16; Luke 15:3-6; John 13:2-9; John 13:34-35; John 15:12; Psalm 40:3; Matthew 5:4; Psalm 30:5; Philippians 4:13; Romans 3:19-28; Ephesians 2:8-9; Titus 2:11; Psalm 23:4, 6; Psalm 73:23; Psalm 145:18; Isaiah 41:9-10; Genesis 9:8-17; Psalm 23:1-3; Hebrews 13:6; Psalm 73:24; Psalm 139:9-10; Psalm 46:11; Psalm 48:14; Exodus 15:13; Isaiah 41:13; 1 John 4:16; 2 Corinthians 1:3-4; Isaiah 66:13; Psalm 71:20-21; Psalm 121:1-2, 5; Isaiah 40:31; Psalm 40:1, 11, 17; John 14:27; Jeremiah 31:13; 2 Corinthians 5:17; Revelation 3:21; Psalm 121:8; 1 John 4:16; John 14:6; John 3:21; Mark 12:28-31; Luke 10:25-28; 1 Peter 4:10; Matthew 25:31-46; Luke 10:1-11; 1 John 3:18; 1Corinthians 10:24; Mark 10:43; Luke 17:5-10; Deuteronomy 15:11-13; Micah 6-8; 1 Samual 12:20; Isaiah 6:8; Romans 3:19-28; Ephesians 2:8-9; Titus 2:11; Luke 18:16.

Chapter 3 Discover the Power of the Service Driven Life

1 John 4:18; 1 John 4:16-17; Luke 15:3-6; Isaiah 55:1-6; Isaiah 43:1; Revelation 3:20; James 4:8; Romans 3:19-28; Ephesians 2:8-9; Hebrews 13:5; Genesis 1:27-28, 31; Jeremiah 1:5; Mark 12:28-30; Matthew 7:20; John 21:17; Philippians 4:13; Isaiah 41:13; Isaiah 40:31; Psalm 121:1-2, 5; Psalm 40:1, 11, 17; Psalm 23:1-3; James 5:16; John 15:12; John 13:34-35; Romans 1:16; Matthew 4:18-22.

Chapter 4 Discover the Joy in the Service Driven Life

John 15:9-11; Psalm 43:4; Psalm 26:2-3; Psalm 16:11; Romans 15:13; Nehemiah 8:10; John 16:5; John 15:12; John 15:9-11; Isaiah 55:12.

Chapter 5 Discover Your Path of Service

Matthew 7:16; Psalm 16:11; Acts 2:28; Exodus 20:1-17; Proverbs 18:21; James 3:5-6; James 3:9; James 4:11-12; Matthew 7:1-5; Matthew 5:1-2; Matthew 7:24-25; Matthew 7:28; Matthew 7:24-27; Psalm 19:14; John 13:34-35; Mark 12:28-31; James 3:1-12; James 4:6; James 4:10; James 4:1-12; James 3:9; Mark 12:28-31; Luke 10:25-28; John 13:34-35; John 15:12, 17; Luke 10:1-11; John 15:12; Luke 10:1-11; 1 John 3:18; Psalm 48:14; James 5:16; Proverbs 15:29; Jeremiah 33:3; John 1:5; Revelation 2:4; Revelation 2:14; Psalm 43:4; Nehemiah 8:10; James 4:8; Isaiah 6:8; Luke 10:29-37; Psalm 100:2; Zephaniah 3:17; John 13:2-9; John 15:17; Mark 1:35; Matthew 6:8; Psalm 145; Psalm 46:1-5; Psalm 145:18; Psalm 145:8-9; John 15:9-11; Psalm 46:1, 7, 11; Psalm 46:10; Acts 2:29, 36; Revelation 3:20; Psalm 46:10-11; Psalm 46:1; Psalm 121:1,2, 8; Psalm 137:4; Romans 3:24; John 3:7; Genesis 9:8-17; John 15:9-11; Psalm 16:11; Acts 2:28; Matthew 25:31-46; Luke 10:29-37.

Chapter 6 Living the Service Driven Life

Psalm 121:1-2; Psalm 121:5-6; Psalm 121:8; Revelation 3:20; John 15:9-12.

APPENDIX 2

Avenues of Service

There is great meaning in the pages that follow; there is great power and there is great joy in these pages. Travel down these avenues now, spend some time considering how others serve—changing the lives of those they touch and their own lives!

Acres of Love

www.acresoflove.org/

Acres of Love is a legally registered South African NPO, which owns and operates homes for abandoned infants and children, providing a non-institutional setting and pristine environment for the infants and children rescued and entrusted into our care. Infants and children live and thrive in de facto families.

Big Brothers Big Sisters of America

www.bbbs.org/site/c.9iILI3NGKhK6F/b.5962345/k.E123/Volunteer_to_ start_something.htm

For more than 100 years, Big Brothers Big Sisters has operated under the belief that inherent in every child is the ability to succeed and thrive in life. As the nation's largest donor and volunteer supported mentoring network, Big Brothers Big Sisters makes meaningful, monitored matches between adult volunteers ("Bigs") and children ("Littles"), ages 6 through 18, in communities across the country.

Being a Big Brother or Big Sister is one of the most enjoyable things you'll ever do. Not to mention one of the most fulfilling. You have the opportunity to help shape a child's future for the better by empowering him or her to achieve. And the best part is it's actually a lot of fun. You and your Little can share the kinds of activities you already like to do.

Play sports together. Go on a hike. Read books. Eat a pizza with extra anchovies. Or just give some advice and inspiration. Whatever it is you enjoy, odds are you'll enjoy it even more with your Little—and you'll be making a life-changing impact.

Boys & Girls Clubs

www.bcga.org

In every community, boys and girls are left to find their own recreation and companionship in the streets. An increasing number of children are at home with no adult care or supervision. Young people need to know that someone cares about them.

Boys & Girls Clubs offer that and more. Club programs and services promote and enhance the development of boys and girls by instilling a sense of competence, usefulness, belonging, and influence. Boys & Girls Clubs are a safe place to learn and grow—all while having fun. It is the place where great futures are started each and every day.

Boy Scouts of America

www.scouting.org/Volunteer.aspx

The Boy Scouts of America relies on dedicated volunteers to promote its mission of preparing young people to make ethical and moral choices over their lifetime by instilling in them the values of the Scout Oath and Scout Law. Today, nearly 1.2 million adults provide leadership and mentoring to Cub Scouts, Boy Scouts, and Venturers.

Through the dedication of these many volunteers, the Boy Scouts of America remains the foremost youth program of character development and values-based leadership training in America.

To these volunteers, Boy Scouts of America say thank you for your dedication to Scouting.

And, to adults who are not currently Scout volunteers, you are invited to become a volunteer and share in the positive experiences of Scouting programs.

Bread for the World

www.bread.org/help/

Bread for the World is a collective Christian voice urging the nation's decision makers to end hunger at home and abroad. God's grace in Jesus

Christ moves these men and women to help neighbors, whether they live in the next house, the next state, or the next continent. Confronting the problem of hunger can seem overwhelming. What can one person do? Plenty. Bread for the World members write personal letters and emails and meet with members of Congress.

Working through churches, campuses, and other organizations, Bread for the World engages more people in advocacy. Each year, Bread for the World invites churches across the country to take up a nationwide Offering of Letters to Congress on an issue that is important to hungry and poor people.

Catholic Charities USA

www.catholiccharitiesusa.org/NetCommunity/Page.aspx?pid=1174
www.catholiccharitiesusa.org/NetCommunity/Page.aspx?pid=2040

Each year, over 200,000 individuals lend their hearts and hands at local Catholic Charities agencies. Volunteers are the backbone of the Catholic Charities network, providing critical support to agencies on the forefront of the economic crisis.

Catholic Charities USA is the national office for local Catholic Charities agencies and affiliates nationwide. Catholic Charities USA provides strong leadership and support to enhance the work of local agencies in their efforts to reduce poverty, support families, and empower communities. Catholic Charities USA's members provide help and create hope for more than 9 million people of all faiths each year.

The Clinebell Institute

http://theclinebellinstitute.org/

The mission of The Clinebell Institute is to offer the community a commitment to serve the whole person by offering professional, affordable pastoral counseling and psychotherapy, educational opportunities for personal growth, and training for pastoral counselors.

Pastoral counseling uses the insights and principles of spirituality, religion, theology, and modern behavioral sciences in working with individuals, couples, families, groups, and institutions toward the achievement of wholeness and health. An important dimension in pastoral counseling different from other approaches to counseling and psychotherapy is the conviction that mental and emotional health is best understood when spiritual, religious, and psychological needs of individuals are addressed.

For more information see the website of the American Association of Pastoral Counselors, www.aapc.org.

Congregational Christian Churches

www.naccc.org/

Bringing together Congregational Christian Churches for mutual care and outreach to our world in the name of Jesus Christ.

Coastal Mountain Youth Academy

www.cmya.org

Coastal Mountain Youth Academy provides an educational and therapeutic setting for adolescents that have struggled in a traditional school environment. A community with a sense of teamwork that stands to solve the problems associated with addiction, abuse, harassment, and self harm. CMYA's programs offer a safe, nurturing, blame free environment which enables students to achieve their full potential.

Ecumenical Lutheran Church in America

www.elca.org

Regardless of age, race, or status in life, members of the Evangelical Lutheran Church in America welcome you to join this community of faith. If you're unfamiliar with this church, some of what you learn may surprise you. The ELCA is an engaged, active body of people who put faith in God into action in millions of ways all over the world.

Service Opportunities: Get involved. Make a difference. Share God's love.

Today's the day. Everywhere you look there is good work waiting to be done. The ELCA and its partners offer a wide range of opportunities to get involved, get your hands dirty, and get to work. From spending a year on the other side of the globe as a mission worker to working as a youth leader at a local congregation to providing comfort and shelter to victims of a natural disaster—there are countless big and small ways that you can help share God's love with the world. In doing so, you may be surprised how God blesses your life, too.

Exchange Club
www.nationalexchangeclub.org

Founded in 1911 in Detroit by businessmen who wanted to "exchange" ideas, the Exchange Club moved its headquarters to Toledo in 1917. For nearly 100 years, its volunteer efforts have supported the needs of the country and of local communities, making it the country's oldest American service organization operating exclusively in this country.

Family Assistance Ministries
www.family-assistance.org

The South Orange County Family Assistance Ministries was founded in 1999 to continue to accommodate the families that the Episcopal Service Alliance could no longer serve.

The first case, in September 1999, provided rental assistance to an individual so eviction could be prevented. Within 30 days, this individual became employed at a major retailer, becoming self-sufficient and a productive member of our community.

Now, Family Assistance Ministries is providing temporary assistance to more than 600 families and individuals.

Feeding America Food Bank
http://feedingamerica.org/take-action/volunteer.aspx

Feeding America Food Bank members help provide low-income individuals and families with the fuel to survive and even thrive. As the nation's leading domestic hunger-relief charity, this network supplies food to more than 37 million Americans each year, including 14 million children and 3 million seniors.

How the Network Works

Feeding America benefits from the unique relationship between its 202 local member food banks at the front lines of hunger relief and the central efforts of its national office.

Each day, hunger is experienced in every community across this country. In fact, this network feeds over 37 million neighbors each year. Ending hunger in America depends on the volunteer work of literally millions of Americans who know that they can make a difference.

There are as many different ways to volunteer as there are individuals and communities across this country. You can help out in your local community through activities such as:

- tutoring kids at your local Kids Cafe
- repackaging donated food for use at food pantries
- transporting food to charitable agencies
- clerical work at the National Office

It's simple—get involved today; and get your family and friends involved. To find opportunities in your area, please contact your local food bank which can be found through the network's website.

Feed My Sheep

http://feedmysheepgulfport.org/category/volunteer/

Feed my Sheep is a non-judgmental, faith based program dedicated to providing nourishment to the homeless, homebound, and needy of the Gulfport area.

Even though there is no "structured religious element" of the Feed My Sheep program, the Christian Spirit is alive and well in this program. When Jesus instructed his disciples to "…feed my sheep," He not only meant physical nourishment, but also spiritual nourishment.

Service is provided on a "no questions asked" basis.

How to get involved:

- Deliver meals through a local church
- Donate and help support this mission financially
- Volunteer your time and touch a life

There are many ways to get involved. Visit Feed My Sheep online—including website or on Facebook or Twitter for volunteer and event updates.

Girl Scouts of America

www.girlscouts.org/for_adults/volunteering/

Be a Girl Scout Volunteer!

What did you do today? As a Girl Scout volunteer, you'll add meaningful days to girls' lives and to your own. Tackle everything from global warming to election reform. Travel to incredible places. Share your personal passions and create experiences together you'll never forget.

Think it's a full-year commitment? Think again. Schedule tight? No problem. There are endless, flexible ways to participate.

Since 1912, Girl Scouts has built girls of "courage, confidence, and character, who make the world a better place." Girl Scout volunteers are a diverse group of women and men whose expertise, skills, interests, and life experiences nurture each girl's individuality and leadership qualities.

Whether you choose to work directly or indirectly with girls on a short-term or long-term basis, you will get all the instruction, guidance, and support you need.

Goodwill Industries International, Inc.

www.goodwill.org/

Goodwill Industries International enhances the dignity and quality of life of individuals, families and communities by eliminating barriers to opportunity and helping people in need reach their fullest potential through the power of work.

For more than a century, volunteers have advanced Goodwill's ability to improve lives, families, and communities. Goodwill recognizes that in order to fulfill its mission, it needs the help and support of those in local communities.

Each of the 165 local Goodwills is led by a board of volunteer leaders who help shape their organization's work to meet the needs of their community.

Valued volunteers contribute their time, knowledge, and support in a variety of ways.

Habitat for Humanity

www.habitat.org

Habitat for Humanity is a nonprofit, ecumenical Christian ministry founded on the conviction that every man, woman, and child should have a decent, safe, and affordable place to live. Building with people in need regardless of race or religion. Welcoming volunteers and supporters from all backgrounds. Former U.S. President Jimmy Carter and his wife Rosalynn are Habitat's most famous supporters. The couple annually leads the Jimmy and Rosalynn Carter Work Project.

Invisible Children

www.invisiblechildren.com/spread-the-word

Invisible Children uses the power of media to inspire young people to help end the longest running war in Africa. The model has proven effective, and hundreds of thousands of people have been called to action through IC films and the volunteers that tour them.

IC is made up of a tireless staff, hundreds of full time volunteers, and thousands of students and supporters. They are young, they are citizens of the world, they are artists, activists, and entrepreneurs. They are using their voices to ask President Obama to spearhead efforts to bring peace to Northern Uganda. They are mobilizing a generation to capture the attention of the international community and make a stand for justice in the wake of genocide.

Kairos Prison Ministry

http://kairosprisonministry.org/

Kairos is an international Christian ministry. Kairos Prison Ministry International, Inc. is the parent organization of a body of ministries operating as chapters that are located in many states and countries addressing the spiritual needs of incarcerated men, women, and children, and to their families and to those who work in the prison environment.

Key Club
www.keyclub.org/discover.aspx

Key Club is an international student-led organization which provides its members with opportunities to provide service, build character, and develop leadership.

Key Club International is the oldest and largest service program for high school students. It teaches leadership through service to others. Members of the Kiwanis International family, Key Club members, build themselves as they build their schools and communities.

Kiwanis International

www.kiwanis.org

Kiwanis International is a global organization of members of every age who are dedicated to changing the world, one child and one community at a time.

Knights of Columbus

www.kofc.org

Thanks to the efforts of Father Michael J. McGivney, Assistant Pastor of St. Mary's Church in New Haven and some of his parishioners, the Connecticut state legislature on March 29, 1882, officially chartered the Knights of Columbus as a fraternal benefit society. The Order is still true to its founding principles of charity, unity, and fraternity.

The Knights was formed to render financial aid to members and their families. Mutual aid and assistance are offered to sick, disabled, and needy members and their families. Social and intellectual fellowship is promoted among members and their families through educational, charitable, religious, social welfare, war relief, and public relief works.

LA Food Bank

www.lafoodbank.org/volunteer/information.aspx

Without volunteers, the Foodbank would not be able to provide food for thousands of hungry people every week. Get together with a social, church, or work group, and spend a day with the LA Food Bank. Learn more about becoming a Food Bank volunteer; contact the volunteer coordinator at (323) 234-3030.

Laura's House www.laurashouse.org

http://laurashouse.org/category.php?catIDdisp=41&PID=womangirl

Our mission: Changing social beliefs, attitudes, and the behaviors that perpetuate domestic violence while creating a safe space in which to empower individuals and families affected by abuse.

For any non-profit organization, volunteerism is essential. Laura's House depends on volunteers to keep all of our programs running smoothly and consistently. Our 150 dedicated volunteers contribute over 10,000 hours per year to our programs.

Fingerprinting is required for all Volunteers and TB Tests for volunteers who work with children. All Volunteers must complete the **40 Hour Training** to work at the Counseling and Resource Center or the Shelter. If you have particular skills in areas that you think could benefit Laura's House, please contact Laura's House.

Lions Club

www.lionsclubs.org

Lions meet the needs of local communities and the world. The 1.35 million members of this volunteer organization in 206 countries and geographic areas are different in many ways, but share a core belief—community is what we make it.

Mariners Church

www.marinerschurch.org

Ordinary people, in love with Jesus, changing the world. Values: Teach God's Word, be God's loving family, remember that every believer is a minister with a ministry, be innovative in our ministry and relevant in our community, be contagious in sharing Jesus Christ.

Mary Erickson Community Housing

http://maryerickson.org/index.htm

Mary Erickson Community Housing (MECH) is a 501 (c) (3) non-profit corporation and designated Community Housing Development Organization serving Southern California. Formed in 1991, MECH owns and operates affordable rental housing in Orange, Riverside and San Bernardino counties. In addition, MECH rehabilitates and develops single family homes to provide homeownership opportunities to income qualified households.

Meals on Wheels

www.mowaa.org/

The Meals on Wheels Association of America is the oldest and largest national organization composed of and representing local, community-based Senior Nutrition Programs in all 50 U.S. states as well as the U.S. Territories. These local programs are the MOWAA Members.

All told, there are some 5,000 local Senior Nutrition Programs in the United States. These programs provide well over one million meals to seniors who need them each day. Some programs serve meals at congregate locations like senior centers, some programs deliver meals directly to the homes of seniors whose mobility is limited, and many programs provide both services.

The Multiple Award-Winning 7th Inning Stretch Middle School Mentoring & Tutoring

www.ocregister.com/news/program-156375-rotarians-kids.html

It is no secret that we have in the United States, and in other countries, an epidemic of children without positive role models. This is no longer a matter of dispute. Every U.S. president since Jimmy Carter—of every political stripe—has talked about this epidemic—single parent families, no parent families, homes with parents not parenting. Many of the kids in Rotary's 7th Inning Stretch mentoring/tutoring programs come from such homes; many have no positive male influence in the home. Some live with a grandmother, an aunt, a single parent. Many, if not most, come from severely dysfunctional families.

It is also no secret that these kids are overwhelmingly at risk for failure, for school drop-out, drugs, crime, gangs. Kids without positive role models will find role models—but they are unlikely to be positive. Nationwide, and around the world, we are reaping the result of the epidemic—this absence of positive role models. Listen to these statistics:

According to the U.S. Department of Justice, the number of juvenile homicide offenders nationwide doubled between 1998 and 2008. During the same period, the murder rate among 14-17 year olds (yes, 14 to 17 year olds!) jumped by 165%. Juvenile arrests increased 117%; gun-related juvenile murder increased 5 fold. 35% of all inmates at the California Youth Authority in Chino, CA believe it is "O.K. to shoot a person if that is what it takes to get something you want." Well, that's just kids in jail, you say? 10% of *all Orange County, California students* polled thought it was "O.K. to shoot a person if that is what it takes to get something you want."

Over 25% of violent crime in California is committed by kids 18 and under. The Young and the Ruthless. If present trends continue, the juvenile arrest rate will double by the year 2014.

What can we do? We can throw up our hands, blame the parents (absent or present). We can whine and moan about it, pour ourselves another drink. Wallow in cynicism and fear. We can build bigger walls around our homes, leave these kids in the lurch and see what happens.

Or we can choose to serve, asking for God's help and guidance. We can choose to make a difference. We can believe that the quality of our own lives, and certainly that of our children, will depend on how well we prepare *all* children for their future.

133

Presbyterian Church USA

www.pcusa.org/

Presbyterians affirm that God comes to us with grace and love in the person of Jesus Christ who lived, died, and rose for us so that we might have eternal and abundant life in Him. As Christ's disciples, called to ministry in His name, we seek to continue his mission of teaching the truth, feeding the hungry, healing the broken, and welcoming strangers. God sends the Holy Spirit to dwell within us, giving us the energy, intelligence, imagination, and love to be Christ's faithful disciples in the world.

More than two million people call the Presbyterian Church (U.S.A.) their spiritual home. Worshiping in 10,000 Presbyterian congregations throughout the United States, they engage the communities in which they live and serve with God's love.

Project Hopeful

www.projecthopeful.org

Project HOPEFUL invites you to join in spreading the truth about HIV/AIDS and children living with the disease. Help fight social stigma; Join the Truth Pandemic.

Rancho Sordo Mudo

http://ranchosordomudo.org/

Rancho Sordo Mudo is a free home and school for deaf children in Baja California, Mexico. Ed and Margaret Everett, the founders of RSM, believed that deaf children could be taught how to read and write, to communicate in sign language, and to learn a trade for their future. More importantly, the goal of the ministry is to teach the children of God's love for them and give them a hope and future.

This has been the work of the ranch for over 40 years.

It is through the prayers, giving, and love from people like you that RSM can continue serving in this special ministry. Throughout the year, service groups and churches visit Rancho Sordo Mudo, bringing needed food, gifts for the kids, and spending time with the kids.

Relay for Life/American Cancer Society

www.relayforlife.org/relay/newtorelay

Relay for Life is the signature fundraising event of the American Cancer Society. There are many components that make up a Relay for Life event, and there are many ways in which you can volunteer and participate in this special event.

To be involved with Relay for Life, you can be a Team Captain or Team Member, a Committee Member, you might be a Survivor or a Caregiver, or you might be an event sponsor, an "Event Day Volunteer," or a donor.

Regardless of your participation, the best way to learn more about how to become involved in your local community is to speak to someone in your local Relay for Life. This webpage provides you with some background information on Relay for Life, how to get involved, and where to turn for resources.

Rotary International

www.rotary.org

Rotary. Humanity in motion.

Devotion to service above self: the excitement, the energy, the vision, the achievement. 1.2 million Rotarians, in the words of Martin Buber "loving powerfully," changing lives; 1.2 million men and women across the face of the planet with something truly extraordinary in common. An organization of leaders, committed to service in your community, in our nation, and in our world, making a difference every single day. Not seeking recognition for past projects, but looking for the next project through which to make a difference in the lives of those in need, of those who hurt. Dividing their service among community service, vocational service, international service, club service.

Youth programs, senior programs, food and toy drives, health related programs, projects to end polio, projects to bring clean water to every child on the planet.

Rotary videos

- You can… You can eradicate polio. You can promote peace. You can feed the hungry. You can help children do better in school. Because you can get involved with Rotary. Learn more at rotary.org. www.youtube.com/watch?v=mKcPFmwXucw

- "The eradication of polio from the face of the planet"
  www.youtube.com/watch?feature=player_embedded&v=ZVfaNJB8x1g

- www.youtube.com/watch?v=G7GdM-rj40k&NR=1

- www.youtube.com/watch?v=YLzUr-fnyFA&NR=1

- "This is a tree that was never chopped down
  To make a crutch that was never needed
  By a child who never got polio"
  www.youtube.com/watch?feature=player_
  detailpage&v=dm5huMgpKmw

- "Come join us"
  www.vimeo.com/17540224

- "We are this close…"
  www.youtube.com/watch?v=6vVyG0TJBWM

- "The last hurdle"
  www.youtube.com/watch?v=nMNPHTV6Z30&feature=player_
  embedded

Rotary programs

End Polio Now

www.rotary.org/en/EndPolio/Pages/ridefault.aspx

After 25 years of hard work, Rotary and its partners are on the brink of eradicating the wild polio virus from the face of the planet. But a strong push is needed now to root it out once and for all. It is a window of opportunity of historic proportions.

Shelterbox

www.shelterbox.org

An international disaster relief charity that delivers emergency shelter, warmth, and dignity to people affected by disaster worldwide. Volunteers are crucial to the work of Shelterbox. Without them, "we would not be able to function."

Interact

www.rotary.org/en/studentsandyouth/youthprograms/interact/pages/ridefault.aspx

Interact is Rotary International's service club for young people ages 12 to 18. Interact Clubs are sponsored by individual Rotary clubs which provide support and guidance, but they are self-governing and self-supporting.

Rotaract

www.rotaract.org

Rotaract is a Rotary-sponsored service club for young men and women ages 18 to 30. Rotaract clubs are either community or university based, and they're sponsored by a local Rotary club. This makes them true "partners in service" and key members of the family of Rotary.

Rotary Youth Leadership Awards Camp

http://ryla5320.org/

Rotary Youth Leadership Awards (RYLA) are all about Rotarians working with youth in leadership development. This is an intensive training/experiential program for 180 high school students in their pivotal junior year who are chosen for their proven or potential leadership abilities. Students participate in an all-expense paid camp, held in Idyllwild Pines, California, for three days. Camp is organized by Rotarians and facilitated by RYLA student Alumni. Students are joined by talented young people from communities throughout the district. RYLA provides a memorable opportunity to learn, grow, have fun, make new friends, and gain a new and improved focus.

What Does RYLA Offer? The core curriculum for RYLA includes the following:

- What Rotary is and what it does for the local and international community
- Importance of communication skills in effective leadership
- Fundamentals of leadership
- Ethics of positive leadership
- Building self-confidence and self-esteem

- Problem-solving and conflict-management
- Elements of Community and Global Citizenship

The 7th Inning Stretch program

The 7th Inning Stretch program for kids at risk provides mentoring and tutoring for middle school students and beyond…to rave reviews—and always heartwarming, sometimes miraculous stories. The core of the program… its mentors and tutors—role models, success models. Rotarians willing to be amazed at how little time it takes to set a new course in a child's life. Rotarians giving their time—an hour per week or more. Giving the gift of time and self that changes lives. Men and women choosing to make a difference in the lives of kids at risk.

Bottom line, the program succeeds because the kids are inspired by Rotarians. The parents and caregivers are inspired by Rotarians—men and women of success, in life and career, men and women of commitment, character, responsibility and…of service. Yes, the kids are inspired, but they cannot be inspired if they do not know you.

Past Rotary International President Frank Devlyn[xciv] said this: "From Seattle to Santiago…from Bogata to Bombay and everywhere in between, the children of the world are waiting. They are the hope of the future but we, you and I, are their hope that the future will be bright."

The 7th Inning Stretch. Community service that changes lives—the lives of the kids, the lives of parents and caregivers, and yes, the lives of those who serve—the mentors and tutors.

For more information on the *7th Inning Stretch*, contact Donald Clinebell at P.O. Box 3808, San Clemente, CA 92674,

Saddleback Church

www.saddleback.com

Saddleback Church serves the Southern California community through more than 200 ministries, eight worship venues, a variety of counseling and support programs, Bible studies and seminars, local and global outreach programs, and a broad network of small groups meeting in local homes. Its purpose is to lead people to Jesus and membership in his family, teach them to worship the Lord and magnify his name, develop them to Christ-like maturity, and equip them for ministry in the church and a mission in the world.

Salvation Army

www.salvationarmyusa.org/usn/www_usn_2.nsf/vw-local/Home

Christianity is synonymous with service for the Salvationist. The distinguishing feature in the religious life of The Salvation Army is active participation by its members. Corps community centers are the focus of the spiritual work and are organized in a military manner, using military terms throughout. The corps building is sometimes known as the "citadel." The pastor serves as an "officer." Members are "soldiers." This sphere of activity is known as the "field." Instead of joining The Salvation Army, members are "enrolled" after signing the "Articles of War." When officers and soldiers die, they are "Promoted to Glory."

Soldiers are disciples of Jesus Christ and are expected to accept responsibility in the work of The Salvation Army. Whenever possible, they participate in Army meetings. Soldiers may teach Sunday-school classes, play musical instruments, join the band, assist the corps officer in visitation among the poor and sick, or aid in general social work. Soldiers abstain from the use of alcoholic beverages, drugs, and tobacco.

Santa Barbara Rape Crisis Center

www.sbrapecrisiscenter.org/05Volunteer/volunteer.html

Volunteers serve as a vital support network, providing over 20,000 hours of service to the community each year.

Crisis intervention advocacy: Requires 60 hours of training plus a one year commitment to the Hotline. Training is held twice per year in English and once per year in Spanish. Female Advocates cover a weekly six hour shift on the 24-hour Hotline and provide crisis counseling, information, advocacy, and accompaniment to survivors of sexual assault and their families and friends. Male and teen advocates also provide support to survivors and their loved ones as well as serving as educators on our Speaker's Bureau.

Save the Children

www.savethechildren.org/site/c.8rKLIXMGIpI4E/b.6540957/k.7CF9/
Volunteer_Opportunities.htm?msource=wexgghp1010

Save the Children is a leading independent organization for children in need with programs in over 120 countries, including the United States. It aims to inspire breakthroughs in the way the world treats children and to achieve immediate and lasting change in their lives by improving their health, education, and economic opportunities. In times of acute crisis, Save the Children mobilizes rapid assistance to help children recover from the effects of war, conflict, and natural disasters. In 2010, the organization improved the lives of over 64 million children in need in the United States and around the world. The goal is to reach more than 74 million children annually by the year 2012. In order to achieve this, Save the Children is actively looking for talented, motivated individuals to join in making a difference in the lives of children worldwide.

Volunteers for Save the Children educate, advocate, and fundraise for the organization from either the Westport, Connecticut or Washington, D.C. offices.

U.S. Volunteer Program

Save the Children highly values the myriad of contributions their volunteers make daily. There are a number of volunteer opportunities available in the Westport, Connecticut, and Washington D.C. offices for individuals looking to make a difference in the lives of children worldwide. Save the Children welcomes and encourages committed individuals to apply as volunteers within all levels of our organization. Volunteer opportunities range from short-term to long-term assignments. They are offered in a variety of areas including, but not limited to, finance, fundraising, marketing and communications, public policy, and social media, as well as research and administrative work.

In order to match your skills, abilities, and interests to the needs of Save the Children, you are invited to submit an application for consideration. A volunteer coordinator will contact you with options for getting involved.

Second Harvest Food Bank

http://feedoc.org/HowToHelp/DONATETIME.aspx

Volunteers bring their hearts and their hands to their work at Second Harvest Food Bank. Your work is vital to the mission of alleviating hunger in the community. Learn more on the Second Harvest website.

One of the most important ways you can get involved in Second Harvest Food Bank is by becoming a hunger relief advocate. Learn more on the Second Harvest website.

Shea Therapeutic Riding Center

www.sheacenter.org

The J.F. Shea Therapeutic Riding Center is dedicated to improving the lives of people with disabilities through therapeutic horse-related programs.

Volunteers willingly give their time, energy, and support to those in need. They have no expectations, but are rewarded by the smiles and exultations of accomplishment from the clients they serve. As part of The Shea Center team, they serve from the heart. Would you like to be a Shea Center volunteer?

Surfers Healing

www.surfershealing.org

Surfers Healing was founded by Israel and Danielle Paskowitz. Their son, Isaiah, was diagnosed with autism at age three. Like many autistic children, he often suffered from sensory overload—simple sensations could overwhelm him. The ocean was the one place where he seemed to find respite.

A former competitive surfer, Israel hit upon an idea—with Isaiah on the front of his surfboard, and Izzy steering from the back, the two spent the day surfing together. Surfing had a profound impact on Isaiah. Israel and Danielle decided they wanted to share this unique therapy with other autistic children. They began to host day camps at the beach where autistic children and their families could be exposed to a completely new experience of surfing.

The Thousand Mile Moms; Acres of Love

www.1000miles-365days.blogspot.com/

The goal of these seven mothers in California is to run 1,000 miles each in 365 days...from Mother's Day 2011 to Mother's Day 2012...to raise awareness for AIDS orphans and funds for the children at Acres of Love in South Africa. Consider sponsoring us per mile or joining our running team.

The United Methodist Church

www.umc.org

The United Methodist Church is an 11-million-strong global church that opens hearts, opens doors, and opens minds through active engagement with our world. John Wesley and the early Methodists placed primary emphasis on Christian living, on putting faith and love into action.

World Vision

www.worldvision.org/content.nsf/getinvolved/activities-and-volunteering?open&dpos=top_drp_GetInvolved_ActivitiesVol

World Vision is a Christian humanitarian organization dedicated to working with children, families, and their communities worldwide to reach their full potential by tackling the causes of poverty and injustice.

Who they serve

World Vision serves close to 100 million people in nearly 100 countries around the world. World Vision serves all people, regardless of religion, race, ethnicity, or gender.

Why they serve

Motivated by faith in Jesus Christ, World Vision volunteers serve alongside the poor and oppressed as a demonstration of God's unconditional love for all people.

Activities & Volunteering

Take the opportunity to share your time and talents in a meaningful way by volunteering at a World Vision office near you—an interactive, walk-through exhibit will transport you into the heart of Africa, and the life of a child.

No endorsement of any charity or organization listed is expressed or implied.

Endnotes

[i] Al-Anon Family Groups, *Courage to Change,* p. 78 (Virginia Beach, VA, 1992) ISBN 0910034796 Albert Schweitzer. German theologian, philosopher, physician and medical missionary (1875-1965).

[ii] Attributed to Mother Teresa (1910-1997) in an interview following her address to the U.N. General Assembly, 10/26/84, *One Strong Resolution: I Will Love.* Generally thought to be Mother Teresa's reading of Galatians 2:20 (I live as Christ who lives in me, and thus I live as a servant) and Romans 14:8 (I live changed because I am the Lord's.)

[iii] Kevin Harris, *Collected Quotes of Albert Einstein,* http://rescomp.stanford. edu/~cheshire/EinsteinQuotes.html, 1995 (may be freely distributed with this acknowledgment) OR In answer to a question asked by the editors of Youth, a journal of Young Israel of Williamsburg, N.Y. Quoted in the N.Y. Times, June 20, 1932, Einstein Archive, 29-041. Albert Einstein (1879-1955) German – Swiss – U.S. Scientist/philosopher.

[iv] Whitman, Walt, *Leaves of Grass,* O Me, O Life, 166. www.gutenberg.org, Book XX, By the Roadside. The Project Gutenberg EBook. 8/24/08, EBook #1322.

[v] Attributed to C. S. Lewis, in a lecture at Oxford University, 1958. Shadowlands, a Richard Attenbourough Film, based on a true story (1993) Savoy Pictures Inc., Anthony Hopkins, Deborah Winger. www.cslewis.drzeus.net "Into the Wardrobe." Intro by step-son Douglas Gresham.

[vi] Taylor, James, *New Moon Shine,* "Copperline"(1991) 9/1/91. 1991 Sony Music Entertainment Inc.

[vii] Attributed to Mother Teresa (1910-1997) in an interview following her address to the U.N. General Assembly, 10/26/84, *One Strong Resolution: I Will Love.* Generally thought to be Mother Teresa's reading of Galatians 2:20 (I live as Christ who lives in me, and thus I live as a servant) and Romans 14:8 (I live changed because I am the Lord's.)

[viii] Lerner, Max. *Touchstones.* Hazelden Educational Materials, Center City, MN 50012 (1991), Page 6/14 Max Lerner (1902-1992) American journalist (syndicated columnist, New York Post) and educator.

[ix] Loosely based on the story "Mr. Misenheimer's Garden" by Charles Kuralt. *On the Road with Charles Kuralt*, page. 34, Fawcett Gold Medal, New York (1985).

[x] D. Elton Trueblood *Touchstones.* Hazelden Educational Materials, Center City, MN 50012 (1991), Page 10/26 D. Elton Trueblood (19090-1994) Noted 20th century American Quaker author and theologian.

[xi] Mother Teresa, *No Greater Love,* (2001), pages 71-71, New World Library, Novato, CA.

[xii] Occasionally, one finds in books about living a "spiritual" life, a dance; a skirting of the edges, if you will. Whether for fear of the concept or fear of alienating potential readers, one finds references not to God, but to a "spiritual center," a "spirit," a "universal spirit," a "source."

These oblique references can be, at best, less than helpful. What is a "source," exactly? A lighted lampshade? A mystical spirit in the night? What I find troublesome about some spiritual "self-help," is the lack of honesty. Does the author believe in God, or not? If not, tell us so...tell us that what we are reading is new age, mystical, re-invented eastern philosophy for the masses. If you do believe in God, it is spiritually and intellectually dishonest not to call Him by name.

In the pages of this book, the use of the word "God" is not an accident. I do not avoid or shy away from the word "God," nor the reality of God and faith in God; the comfort of God. God is present where love and caring are present – and *that* is central to the service driven life.

If (or perhaps more accurately "when") we truly believe that God walks beside us at all times, we cannot experience fear and doubt. It is not that "source" or "spirit" walks beside us. Or that a "spiritual center" walks beside us. Or that a lighted lampshade walks beside us. It is that *God* walks beside us. He knows my name and He calls it. (Jeremiah 1:5.) And I call Him by his name. (Isaiah 43:1) And that is good news! When we decline "God," we retain a hedge against a bet, an element of fear, a refusal of Faith.

[xiii] *Miracle on 34th Street*, A John Hughes Production, 2000, A Les Mayfield Film, 20th Century Fox.

[xiv] Rabindranth Tagore, Indian poet (1861-1941). *Touchstones.* Hazelden Educational Materials, Center City, MN 50012 (1991), Page 12/20.

xv Pablo Casals, Cellist. (1876-1973.) *Touchstones.* Hazelden Educational Materials, Center City, MN 50012 (1991), Page 6/01.

xvi Walter Issacson, *Einstein; His Life and Universe, chapter 17, Einstein's God,* pp. 385-387 (2007) Simon & Schuster, N.Y., N.Y.

xvii Einstein, Albert *The World As I See It, p. 24-28,* Citadel Press, Secaucus, NJ (No copyright registration shown in the Citadel Press publication.)

xviii Collins, Francis S., *The Language of God; A Scientist Presents Evidence for Belief,* p. 225, Free Press, Division of Simon & Schuster (2006).

xix Collins, Francis S., *The Language of God; A Scientist Presents Evidence for Belief,* p. 225, Free Press, Division of Simon & Schuster (2006).

xx Henri Nouwen. *The Return of the Prodigal Son.* p. 12, Bantom Doubleday Dell Publishing Group, N.Y. N.Y. (1992).

xxi Peter Kreeft. *Prayer: The Great Conversation.* p. 13, Ignatius Press, San Francisco. (1991).

xxii Leslie Bianco, *In the Company of Prayer, Workday Reflections For Those Who Lead By Example,* 2010 Q1 Publishing. Daily meditations at www.CompanyofPrayer.com A wonderful resource to seek God and let Him find you in prayer.

xxiii *The Father Will Dance Over You,* Arranged by Mark Hayes, Hinshaw Music, Inc. (1983) Chapel Hill, N.C. 27514.

xxiv A.J. Russell, Editor, *God Calling,* p. 8/28, Barbour Publishing, Inc. Uhrichsville, OH44683.

xxv *Alcoholics Anonymous:The Story of How Many Thousands of Men and Women Have Recovered From Alcoholism,* 4th Ed., 2001Alcoholics Anonymous World Services, Inc., New York, NY.

xxvi *Alcoholics Anonymous:The Story of How Many Thousands of Men and Women Have Recovered From Alcoholism,* p. 59, 4th Ed., 2001Alcoholics Anonymous World Services, Inc., New York, NY.

[xxvii] *Alcoholics Anonymous: The Story of How Many Thousands of Men and Women Have Recovered From Alcoholism*, p. 57, 4th Ed., 2001 Alcoholics Anonymous World Services, Inc., New York, NY.

[xxviii] Ojibway, *Touchstones*. Hazelden Educational Materials, Center City, MN 50012 (1991), Page 12/3. The **Ojibwe** (also **Ojibwa** or **Ojibway**) or **Chippewa** (also **Chippeway**) are among the largest groups of Native Americans north of Mexico. In the United States, they are the fourth largest Native American population.

[xxix] Collins, Francis S., *The Language of God; A Scientist Presents Evidence for Belief,* p. 225 , Free Press, Division of Simon & Schuster (2006)

[xxx] The journal of John Wesley, May 24, 1738. Spanning some fifty-five years, John Wesley's voluminous *Journal* records his daily tribulations experienced in traveling the length and breadth of the British Isles in the 18th century.

[xxxi] A.J. Russell, Editor, *God Calling*, Barbour Publishing, Inc. Uhrichsville, OH44683

[xxxii] http://alphamom.com/family-fun/holidays/family-day-share-a-meal-best-ideas-for-mealtime-with-kids/http://www.time.com/time/magazine/article/0,9171,1200760,00.html.

[xxxiii] Footprints in the Sand.
Three people claim authorship of this wonderful piece. http://www.wowzone.com/fprints.htm

[xxxiv] *Webster's New World Dictionary of American English*, Prentice Hall 3rd Ed. 1994, p. 1226.

[xxxv] *The United Methodist Hymnal*, "The Church's One Foundation" p. 545, The United Methodist Publishing House. 1989 Nashville, TN.

[xxxvi] St. Francis of Assisi. (1181-1226.) This timeless quotation is in the public domain; it is over 800 years old. St. Francis of Assisi was an Italian Catholic friar and preacher. He founded the men's Franciscan Order. Saint Francis is one of the most venerated religious figures in history. He is a wonderful source for great prayer. Prayer that we hear in many settings is often taken, without attribution. from St. Francis. Here is the best example of that, a prayer that is both timeless and uplifting:

"Lord, make me an instrument of your peace.
Where there is hatred, let me sow love;

where there is injury, pardon;
where there is doubt, faith;
where there is despair, hope;
where there is darkness, light;
and where there is sadness, joy.

Grant that I may not so much seek
to be consoled as to console;
to be understood as to understand;
to be loved as to love.
For it is in giving that we receive;
it is in pardoning that we are pardoned;
and it is in dying that we are born to eternal life. Amen."

xxxvii There is no biblical support for the statement that those who do not serve lose their eternal rewards. The closest one can get to that is found in Luke, just before the story of the good Samaritan. There, "an expert in the law" asks Jesus "what must I do to inherit eternal life?" Jesus' answer: The two greatest commandments; "Love the Lord your God with all your heart, mind, soul and strength; love your neighbor as yourself." (Luke 10:25-27.)

xxxviiii http://wikipedia.org/wiki/Amazing_Grace

xxxix *The United Methodist Hymnal,* "Amazing Grace" p. 378, The United Methodist Publishing House. 1989 Nashville, TN *Hymns for the Family of God* "Amazing Grace" p. 106-107 Brentwood Benson Publishing (1976)

xl Wintley Phipps is the President of the U.S. Dream Academy, and an astonishing Bass talent. His vocal talents are extraordinary and inspired. http://www.youtube.com/watch?v=DMF_24cQqT0

xli *The United Methodist Hymnal,* "Amazing Grace" p. 378, The United Methodist Publishing House. 1989 Nashville, TN *Hymns for the Family of God* "Amazing Grace" p. 106-107 Brentwood Benson Publishing (1976)

xlii This man of service prefers to remain anonymous in his service, but has given permission for this story to be told. God bless him and his work – which includes many surgeries every year, without charge, in third world countries around the globe.

xliii Kiel and Carolyn Twietmeyer , on *Hour of Power.* www.projecthopeful.org/media1?pid=8]

[xliv] Gregorian chant is the central musical tradition of western Christianity. It is named after Pope Gregory, Bishop of Rome from 590 to 604, who is traditionally credited for having ordered the simplification and cataloging of music assigned to specific celebrations in the church calendar. The resulting body of music is the first to be notated in a system ancestral to modern musical notation. Public domain.

[xlv] A.J. Russell, Editor, *God Calling*, p. 3/25, Barbour Publishing, Inc. Uhrichsville, OH44683

[xlvi] Isaac Bashevis Singer. Touchstones, Hazelden Educational Materials, Center City M N 50012 (1991) Page 7/12 Polish American author noted for his short stories He was one of the leading figures in the Yiddish literary movement, and received the Nobel Prize in Literature in 1978. He is also well known for the memoir of his life, A Day Of Pleasure.

[xlvii] Henry David Thoreau (1817- 1862) was an American poet, author and philosopher. This quotation is from *Civil Disobedience and Other Essays:Collected Essays of Henry David Thoreau.* (2005) Digreads.com Publishing, Stilwell, KS.

[xlviii] Al-Anon Family Groups, *Courage to Change*, p.39 (Virginia Beach, VA, 1992) ISBN 0910034796. Oscar Wilde (1854-1900.) Irish writer and poet. After writing in different forms throughout the 1880s, he became one of London's most popular playwrights in the early 1890s.

[xlix] Jeffrey Marx, *The Long Snapper; A Second Chance,* Inside cover sleeve and chapter 20, HarperCollins, 2009, N.Y. N.Y. Mark is a Pulitzer Prize winning author.

[l] Al-Anon Family Groups, *Courage to Change*, p. 9 (Virginia Beach, VA, 1992) ISBN 0910034796. Carl Jung. (1875-1961) Swiss psychiatrist and founder of analytical psychology. Considered the first modern psychiatrist to view the human psyche as "by nature religious" and make it the focus of exploration.

[li] Wayne Dyer. This is a frequent theme in Dyer's books. If you want more, start with *The Power of Intention*, 2004, Hay House, Carlsbad, CA. Page 63 et seq.

[lii] Bruce McCombs, CPCC. a true man of service, has given his permission for the use of this story of the joy of mentoring. In Bruce's words: 'Whatever we think about and set the intention for is what we manifest! It is in our prayers, our beliefs, our actions that this manifestation is set in motion.' "http://brucemccombsenterprises.com"

liii St. Francis of Assisi. (1181-1226.) This timeless quotation is in the public domain; it is over 800 years old.

liv Brian Wren, 1969, United Methodist Hymnal, p. 192, "There's a Spirit in the Air".

lv Janet provided her dialogue for this book with written permission to the author.

lvi This wonderful story was told in the movie *Regarding Henry,* a Mike Nichols Film, based on a true story. Written by Jeffrey Abrams. A Paramount Pictures release. 1991.

lvii Attributed to C. S. Lewis, in a lecture at Oxford University, 1958. *Shadowlands,* a Richard Attenbourough Film, based on a true story (1993) Savoy Pictures Inc., Anthony Hopkins, Deborah Winger. www.cslewis.drzeus.net "Into the Wardrobe." Intro by step-son Douglas Gresham.

lviii A.J. Russell, Editor, *God Calling,* p. 4/18, Barbour Publishing, Inc. Uhrichsville, OH

lix A.J. Russell, Editor, *God Calling,* p. 5/17, Barbour Publishing, Inc. Uhrichsville, OH

lx Kevin Harris, *Collected Quotes of Albert Einstein,* http://rescomp.stanford.edu/~cheshire/EinsteinQuotes.html, 1995 (may be freely distributed with this acknowledgment)

lxi My friend has given her permission to use this story in this book.

lxii The name of this wonderful mentor has been changed. He prefers to remain anonymous in his service, but has given permission for the use of this story of the joy of mentoring.

lxiii Josh's mentor, Robert, has given his permission to use this story in this book.

lxiv Josh's mentor, Robert, has given his permission to use this story in this book.

lxv Kevin's mentor is the author of this book.

lxvi My son's writing and this story are used with his permission and participation. Thank you, Brennan. You and your sister, Tessa, make me so very proud.

[lxvii] Whitman, Walt, *Leaves of Grass*, O Me, O Life, 166. www.gutenberg.org, Book XX, By the Roadside. The Project Gutenberg EBook. 8/24/08, EBook #1322.

[lxviii] Mother Teresa, *In My Own Words*, page 51 and 75, Ligouri Publishing, Liguouri, Missouri (1996)

[lxix] J. Russell, Editor, *God Calling*, p. 4/16, Barbour Publishing, Inc. Uhrichsville, OH

[lxx] *Webster's New World Dictionary of American English*, Prentice Hall 3rd Ed. 1994, p. 1191.

[lxxi] This inspiring story was told in the movie *Regarding Henry*, a Mike Nichols Film, based on a true story. Written by Jeffrey Abrams. A Paramount Pictures release. 1991.

[lxxii] J. Russell, Editor, *God Calling*, p. 4/16, Barbour Publishing, Inc. Uhrichsville, OH

[lxxiii] St. Francis of Assisi. (1181-1226.) This timeless quotation is in the public domain; it is over 800 years old.

[lxxiv] Coelho, Paul, *By the River Piedra I Sat Down and Wept.* p. 145 (1998) Harper Collins Publishers, N.Y. N.Y. Brazilian novelist and lyricist.

[lxxv] This story is about the author. Thank you for letting me share it with you.

[lxxvi] *Les Miserables, The Musical.* (1985) Music by Claude-Michel Schonberg. Lyrics by Alain Boublil. Based on the 1862 novel *Les Miserables,* By Victor Hugo. Simon & Brown 2011 First copyright: 1862

[lxxvii] Used with the written permission of John Bell, Esq., lawyer and juggler extraordinaire.

[lxxviii] J. Russell, Editor, *God Calling*, p. 5/31, Barbour Publishing, Inc. Uhrichsville, OH

[lxxix] Peter Kreeft. *Prayer: The Great Conversation.* p. 13, Ignatius Press, San Francisco. (1991).

[lxxx] LW 35:254 *Luther's Works* , 55 volumes, Helmut Lehmann, ed., Fortress & Concordia, 1955-1986.

[lxxxi] The phrase "religion that hurts" was written by Howard Clinebell, Ph.D, an ordained Methodist minister; one of the pioneers in the pastoral psychology and counseling movement; the founding professor of pastoral counseling at the Claremont School of Theology; founder of The Clinebell Institute in Claremont. http://www.theclinebellinstitute.org/ The phrase "religion that hurts" is taken from an outline for a book Dr. Clinebell intended to write – it was tentatively titled "Religion That Heals, Religion That Hurts." The book would have been added to his list of over 20 published books. In 2004, there came to Howard Clinebell, my father, "not the final sleep, but the final awakening." I miss you, Dad.

The phrase "not the final sleep, but the final awakening" is sometimes attributed to Sir Walter Scott (1771-1835), Scottish author and poet. William J. Bennett's book, *The Book of Virtues*, suggests that the origin of the phrase is actually found in the John Donne poem *Death, Be Not Proud.* John Donne (1572-1631) was an English poet, lawyer, and priest. (William Bennett, The Book of Virtues, (1993) (Bennett's commentary preceding John Donne *Death, Be Not Proud),* Simon & Schuster, N.Y., N.Y.)_

[lxxxii] *Teachers as Spiritual Leaders and Theologians*
General Board of Discipleship of The United Methodist Church, 2010. Cokesbury.

[lxxxiii] George Koehler. *The United Methodist Member's Handbook.*, pp. 78-79. Cokesbury. 10/97 Disciples Publications.

[lxxxiv] *The Talmud,* Talmud Brakhot 17a. The Talmud is the central text of mainstream Judaism.

[lxxxv] J. Russell, Editor, *God Calling,* p. 4/8, Barbour Publishing, Inc. Uhrichsville, OH

[lxxxvi] The Orange County Register, Dec. 30, 2006, Part 2, Page 2. Copyright Orange County Register Communications, Santa Ana, CA

[lxxxvii] Appendix 2 to this book.

[lxxxviii] J. Russell, Editor, *God Calling,* p. 9/26, Barbour Publishing, Inc. Uhrichsville, OH

[lxxxix] Whitman, Walt, *Leaves of Grass,* O Me, O Life, 166. www.gutenberg.org, Book XX, By the Roadside. The Project Gutenberg EBook. 8/24/08, EBook #1322.

[xc] J. Russell, Editor, *God Calling*, p. 4/26, Barbour Publishing, Inc. Uhrichsville, OH

[xci] Al-Anon Family Groups, *Courage to Change*, p. 65 (Virginia Beach, VA, 1992) ISBN 0910034796

[xcii] J. Russell, Editor, *God Calling*, p. 8/21, Barbour Publishing, Inc. Uhrichsville, OH

[xciii] Mother Teresa. *No Greater Love.* page 48, New World Publishing, Novato, CA 1989. Also www.goodread.com/author/quotes/838305.

[xciv] Frank Devlyn was Rotary International President in 2000-2001. This quotation was delivered at a speech to the Rotary International Convention in the year 2000. This dynamic leader and inspirational speaker is truly a man of service. His website can be found at: http://www.frankdevlyn.org/

ABOUT THE AUTHOR

Donald Clinebell is a distinguished lawyer, author, powerful speaker, a man of faith and a man of service. He is a Phi Beta Kappa graduate of Pomona College and UCLA School of Law. He is a former Deputy Attorney General for the State of California and founding partner in The Clinebell Law Firm (www.theclinebelllawfirm.com).

Donald is a life-long Methodist and a "preacher's kid." He is the youngest son of Dr. Howard Clinebell, Ph.D and Dr. Charlotte Ellen, Ph.D. His father was an ordained Methodist Minister for nearly 60 years, Professor of Pastoral Counseling at the Claremont School of Theology for nearly 35 years; a world renowned author; a pioneer in the pastoral care and counseling movement; a founding President of the American Association of Pastoral Counselors ("AAPC").

In the words of Dr. Steve Shim, AAPC Diplomate: "The Service Driven Life is an important work, a must-read companion to several of the writings of the late Dr. Howard Clinebell. Dr. Clinebell would have been much affirming of his son's writing and this book."

In Donald's own words: "My father, Howard Clinebell, instilled in me a love of learning and writing. Sadly, he did not see the book come to fruition before his "final awakening". But during my work on the book, I have often felt his presence—which has increased both my faith and my love for him."

Charlotte Ellen is a psychotherapist who works with sexual assault survivors. She has written extensively on the relationship of the sexes, and about working with children.

"From the Dedication of The Service Driven Life: "My parents, Howard and Charlotte, from the beginning nourished my faith and taught me that I am filled with the capacity to love and to serve."

His avenues of service include:

- Through home & family
- Through the practice of law, The Clinebell Law Firm
- Through writing and speaking

- Volunteer counsel to the Orange County District of the United Methodist Church and a member of the Annual Conference Lawyers Committee, representing pro bono some 50 churches.

- Charter member of the San Clemente Sunrise Rotary Club ("SCSRC"). Donald served as President of the Club in 1995-96. During his tenure, the SCSRC grew in membership by a full 75% and won seven District-wide awards and two international awards.

- Assistant Governor, District 5320, Rotary International. Mr. Clinebell is a frequent keynote speaker at Rotary events.

- Featured speaker and trainer at Presidents Elect Training Seminar ("PETS")—annual training seminar for incoming Rotary Presidents. In that capacity, Mr. Clinebell has had a major hand in training nearly 8000 Rotary Presidents.

- Founding Chair of the 7th Inning Stretch Middle School Mentoring & Tutoring Program for kids at risk. Founded in 1995, the program has touched the lives of thousands of kids. Community service that truly changes lives—the lives of the students, of the parents/caregivers, and the lives of the mentors and tutors. The program has received multiple awards, including the California Golden Bell, a statewide award recognizing excellence in community-based school programs. To learn more about the program, please visit http://articles.ocregister.com/2006-03-17/cities/24776692_1_rotarians-program-rotary-international

- Member of the San Clemente Dons, a service organization whose membership is made up of honored and respected civic leaders.

- Multiple Paul Harris Fellow and Paul Harris Society Member (recognizing contributions to the Rotary International Foundation, which Foundation has funded over two billion polio vaccines since 1987).

- Praise Team (vocal) member: Palisades United Methodist Church & St. Andrews by the Sea United Methodist Church. Our Saviors Lutheran Church. Sunday school teacher, Third through Fifth grades.

Donald's scholastic awards include membership in Phi Beta Kappa, the Mary Ford Bacon Prize in Government, Pomona College Scholar, Life Member, California Scholastic Federation; Biography: Who's Who in California.

Aside from his other talents, Donald is also an accomplished baritone and pianist. He lives in San Clemente with his wonderful family, Bonnie, Brennan, and Tessa.

Donald in His Own Words

Service is no longer a question. It is who I am. I strive mightily to "…live as a servant, and thereby I am changed." (Mother Teresa)

I am so richly blessed, in so many ways – through home and family, those most precious in my life; through "neighbor," those whose path I have crossed and will cross. In vocation, I am also truly blessed. I have been given a great gift: The opportunity to serve others through the law and the legal profession. And now, I have been given the opportunity to serve others with the message of *The Service Driven ™ Life*. I thank God for entrusting to me the message of this book, and allowing me to share it with you. May you be truly blessed by the meaning, power and joy of *The Service Driven™ Life!*"

THE STORY
BEHIND THE BOOK

I have been a life-long Methodist and "preacher's kid." I am the youngest
son of Dr. Howard Clinebell, Ph.D and Dr. Charlotte Ellen, Ph.D., one of
three children. My father was an ordained Methodist Minister for nearly
60 years; Professor of Pastoral Counseling at the Claremont School of
Theology for nearly 35 years; a world-renowned author; a pioneer in the
pastoral care and counseling movement; and a founding President of the
American Association of Pastoral Counselors ("AAPC"). My mother is a
psychotherapist who works with sexual assault survivors; she will leave a
lasting legacy of strength, wisdom and inspiration in that field. She has also
written extensively on the relationship of the sexes and about working with
children.

What a family DNA you might be thinking! And you are right.

As you will see when you read *The Service Driven™ Life*, the book itself
is a product of my own life experience—and God moving in my life. It is
also a product of a simple, but profound, conversation with my father in the
Fall of 2004. It was the last year of my father's life. I sat at his bedside, as I
did many nights in those last days. As I sat, I helped Dad with his supper.
And I shared with him that which I believed was in me to write. I had
never written a book, although I considered myself a writer. I described to
him a book about a life; a life centered around, and driven by, service. A
life driven by service to others in home and family, vocation, and in service
to "neighbor," both literal and biblical. A book grounded in solid theology
and biblical teaching, but also a personal story of renewal—from despair
to hope, from darkness to light, from doubt to faith, from sadness to great
joy! My father listened attentively, nodding gently, but did not speak. As we
finished supper, we sat together in the quiet.

After supper, the gloaming turned to dark and I read to Dad from a
favorite daily reader. Sleep seemed next, and I prepared to depart for the
night. But as I turned to go, Dad stirred and waved at me to return to his
bedside. I sat. He smiled at me and said this: "Donald, you must write

that book." He turned upon his side and he slept—a sleep he would later describe as restful and peaceful. I left, and I too spent a restful and peaceful night.

It was that night that I came to know that I would one day write this book; *The Service Driven ™ Life: Discover Your Path to Meaning, Power, and Joy!*

ADDITIONAL RESOURCES

Donald Clinebell "Live"

Donald is much in demand as a motivational and keynote speaker and lecturer in the fields of leadership in service, mentoring and tutoring programs, grief and loss, and the service driven life. To learn more about Donald's keynote speaking, lectures, full and half day seminars, and to see reviews of his lectures and other presentations, please visit www. theclinebelllawfirm.com/motivational_speaker.html.

The Service Driven Life Lecture Series

In a powerful live lecture, Donald explores The Service Driven Life. For more information, write P.O. Box 3808, San Clemente, CA 92674-3808.

Additional Resources/Group Study

Now that you have been introduced to the joy of living a service driven life, take the next step ... don't just read about the service driven life, LIVE IT! I will show you how in more detail. Order your copy of:

The Service Driven Life Journal—a simple and painless guide to helping you live outside yourself; helping to keep you service driven and on your path to meaning, power and joy!

The Service Driven Life 6-week challenge—this is an ideal small-group study that can be done in a home group, Sunday school class, community service project, weekend retreat or any other format that suits your schedule.

IF YOU'RE A FAN OF THIS BOOK, PLEASE TELL OTHERS...

- Write about *The Service Driven Life* on your blog, Twitter, MySpace, and Facebook page.

- Suggest *The Service Driven Life* to friends.

- When you're in a bookstore, ask them if they carry the book. The book is available through all major distributors, so any bookstore that does not have *The Service Driven Life* in stock can easily order it.

- Write a positive review of *The Service Driven Life* on www.amazon.com.

- Send my publisher, HigherLife Publishing, suggestions on Web sites, conferences, and events you know of where this book could be offered at media@ahigherlife.com.

- Purchase additional copies to give away as gifts.

CONNECT WITH ME...

To learn more about *The Service Driven Life*, please contact me at:

Donald Clinebell

www.theservicedrivenlife.com

donald@theservicedrivenlife.com

You may also contact my publisher directly:

HigherLife Publishing

400 Fontana Circle

Building 1 – Suite 105

Oviedo, Florida 32765

Phone: (407) 563-4806

Email: media@ahigherlife.com